BEHIND AND BEFORE

T0371448

Je fus entraîné vers les sciences historiques, petites sciences conjecturales qui se défont sans cesse après s'être faites, et qu'on négligera dans cent ans. On voit poindre, en effet, un âge où l'homme n'attachera plus beaucoup d'intérêt à son passé. Je crains fort que nos écrits de précision de l'Académie des inscriptions et belles-lettres, destinés à donner quelque exactitude à l'histoire, ne pourrissent avant d'avoir été lus. C'est par la chimie à un bout, par l'astronomie à un autre, c'est surtout par la physiologie générale que nous tenons vraiment le secret de l'être, du monde, de Dieu, comme on voudra l'appeler. Le regret de ma vie est d'avoir choisi pour mes études un genre de recherches qui ne s'imposera jamais et restera toujours à l'état d'intéressantes considérations sur une réalité à jamais disparue. Mais, pour l'exercice et le plaisir de ma pensée, je pris certainement la meilleure part.

E Renan, *Souvenirs d'enfance et de jeunesse,*
1883, p 263.

BEHIND AND BEFORE

TWO ESSAYS ON THE RELATION OF
HISTORY POLITICS AND
EUGENIST WARNINGS.

W E HEITLAND MA

CAMBRIDGE
AT THE UNIVERSITY PRESS
1924

CAMBRIDGE UNIVERSITY PRESS
Cambridge, New York, Melbourne, Madrid, Cape Town,
Singapore, São Paulo, Delhi, Mexico City

Cambridge University Press
The Edinburgh Building, Cambridge CB2 8RU, UK

Published in the United States of America by Cambridge University Press, New York

www.cambridge.org
Information on this title: www.cambridge.org/9781107625587

First published 1924
First paperback edition 2013

A catalogue record for this publication is available from the British Library

ISBN 978-1-107-62558-7 Paperback

PREFACE

I T is customary to praise books and sentiments as being original. Yet I have known a fashionable and gifted critic cite as evidence of a great author's originality an expression borrowed directly from a predecessor. It stood already noted as such in my interleaved copy, and my discovery was not itself new. All students must have, I suspect, many such experiences: a few may have gone astray in much the same manner: I have.

So too with books. Novelty is often no more than a restatement of old opinions from a slightly different point of view. Is it the worse for that? In a long course of very miscellaneous reading I have become more and more distrustful of sparkling paradox, more tolerant of platitudes. And in dealing with matters of human history and politics I do not think that this conclusion is on my part original or even eccentric. The burden of proof seems to lie on those whose attitude inclines toward revolutionary treatment of such topics. Therefore in dressing up old materials in various combinations I stand unashamed. A vast amount of fumbling is in this troubled age going on among those who take interest in political subjects: and academic teaching, carried on by hard-worked teachers, leaves to a number of distinguished specialists little leisure for reconsideration of their general aims.

That I am confessedly dealing in platitudes does not mean that I have taken opinions ready-made out of the works of my betters and patched them together with a paste-brush. As I have said below, the phenomena of

the war-time set me thinking; wondering how public
men with any insight into the present or any knowledge
of the past could act as they were acting from day to
day. They were however, true to themselves, doing as
they had been doing in earlier years. We had suffered
them then: was it fair to complain of them now?

Stray facts that leaked out soon betrayed the truth
that what the ordinary citizen could detect was but a
small part of the confusion that reigned in administrative
circles. Apart from the army-organization reforms of
Lord Haldane, good but inadequate to the strain of the
moment, nothing save the Fleet was really ready: all
things had been left to worry along on the tacit assumption that no pressing need for organizing our resources
was likely to arise at brief notice. In short, the people
had been lulled into fancied security by the time-serving
reticence of some of their leaders and the misrepresenta-
tions of others. What it cost us in unnecessary bloodshed
and huge waste of money to do everything in frantic
haste against a fully prepared enemy, we are just beginning to understand. How near we came to disastrous
failure, those only know who were then behind the
scenes.

As cool observation became possible after years of
suspense and alarm, I saw more and more clearly that
our pitiful confusion during the war was nothing more
than the cruel exposure of our shortcomings in the time
of peace. Moreover it was only too evident that as a
nation we had not learnt our lesson: as before, we were
deluding ourselves with unrealities. Naturally there

arose the question, is this the inevitable result of what is called popular government? Granting that a perfect adaptation of measures to needs is more than human imperfection allows us to expect, could we not, being what we are, manage our public affairs somewhat better than we do? Is not our success in the world mainly due to the use and development of quite different qualities in our private affairs? Does not that difference consist in the greater value attached to actual qualification for performance of this or that duty, ultimately to education in the widest sense? If so, what have we been doing, and what ought we to do, in the way of equipping citizens, both leaders and followers, for the duties of public life?

In answer, I have attempted to indicate the dangers that beset our haphazard system or lack of system, starting from the assumption that, with men as they are, the operations of popular government must and will have a certain haphazard character. I have tried to discover how far and in what ways a knowledge of past history can be of use and benefit to a functioning citizen. Abler pens than mine have long insisted on its usefulness: that we may perhaps take for granted. But as to the way in which such knowledge can operate usefully there is less general agreement. I have tried to think my own way to a conclusion from consideration of important illustrative cases. This provisionally reached, I consulted a large number of good authorities, reading with a strong bias inclining me to attach most weight to the views of those writers who had themselves had experience of the responsibilities of public duty. My reading has been discursive and various, and it has modified little, and fortified much, in the conclusions at which I had arrived.

The method followed is naturally productive of platitude, for I did not and do not suppose that I have a stock of real novelties to vend. There is nothing in what I have written that makes pretence to be 'arresting', as the modern cant phrase has it. But, however stale my thesis may be, there remains the fact that we need more trained intelligence in our public policy, and that this need seems now (1923) quite as pressing as it was in past years. Now it is tacitly assumed, and sometimes openly asserted, that the supply to meet this demand must to a great extent come from the Universities. And yet we may note that men of full academic training now and then shew themselves liable to the same sort of errors as those not so trained. Therefore I have timidly ventured to ask whether this academic training may not be abdicating some of its usefulness by attempting too much.

The recent growth of biological criticism applied to sociological and political questions is a phenomenon of grave importance. To a non-scientific reader it is in its present stage apt to bring unqualified alarm: in a sympathetic and impressionable mind it may breed a sort of moral paralysis. It is however not irrelevant to remember that any medical treatise is apt to alarm the unprofessional reader, making him fancy himself the victim of many maladies in incurable forms, while he

Preface ix

puts little trust in rules or suggestions of treatment. Now in this politico-biological inquiry we have as yet only attempts at social pathology pure and simple: of a therapeutic scheme we have only a passing hint here and there. And such hints only amount to this, that human conduct must be different from what it is now. Perhaps no general conclusion is so ancient as this. But the fact of its being now reached by genuine men of Science gives it new point and urgency. It is the therapeutic side that calls for development; for a people that idly lapses into chronic pessimism is lost. I have therefore tried to indicate not only certain criticisms in which some exaggeration may possibly be suspected, but also some points in which the criticism may be felt to lack completeness. For the future of the human race, and the British part of it in particular, seems to be at stake, if the Biologist critics are right, and it would be madness to waste effort in misdirected striving after what is ideally desirable but not feasible.

That such inquiries as these have a bearing on the value of historical studies, I have no doubt. The fascination of a purely antiquarian interest is great, and it shews no sign of slackening. But meanwhile the world is moving on to better or worse. If History is not to become a record of hopes unfulfilled and errors unredeemed, historians will have to keep an eye on the imminent as well as on the past. This they are beginning to do, influenced by social and anthropological researches as well as by the political phenomena of peace or war. The economic point of view is already fully recognized:

even ethical considerations now and then put in a timid claim. But surely there is a long road to travel yet. In particular, the behaviour of mankind in masses and groups is now being studied as not identical with that of the same number taken as individuals. It is found to have special characteristics, and philosophers are aiming at discovering the principles on which a sort of Psychology of Peoples can be founded. This movement is at present in its infancy, but no one can tell how far it may be destined to go. At all events it is closely connected with the study of history, and on historical study as a source of equipment for statesmen and citizens it may exercise an immense influence. Already it shews itself boldly in the many critical utterances of recent writers on Germany old and new. In this case they have enjoyed exceptionally full opportunities of tracing notable effects to adequate causes. But they will not, can not, stop there; and Russia (not to mention minor states) is already furnishing them with rich and significant material.

I hope therefore that considerations relative to the use of history may, however stale to the expert eye, not be irrelevant in the present atmosphere of world-problems, when self-government is on its trial in many countries. And the mention of self-government reminds me that the use of practical means is often quite as important as agreement on desirable ends. In this connexion I have ventured to offer a few remarks on the efforts of some religious bodies to join forces for the promotion of human welfare, and to express some doubts as to the probable effectiveness of their present methods. This I do with much diffidence, but I could not shirk it altogether.

The Appendices are devoted to the consideration of several topics which seemed to require special treatment. That on *Body Politic and Body Natural* is a gleaning of the opinions of a number of highly qualified judges on a question of theory important to students of History. Perhaps I need not apologize for dealing at some length with the views of certain American writers on important problems of national life and welfare. In treating of such questions they are more free than Europeans, less hampered by the pressure of stale conditions inherited from a tangled past. The United States may stand aloof from Europe sick and suffering; Europe, and Great Britain above all, cannot ignore the experiences and action of the United States.

But I must apologize for the length of this Preface. The structure of the book seemed to call for some sort of explanation. I have only to record my thanks to Mr E A Benians for reading the manuscript and for giving me kindly comfort and advice.

W E H

November 1923.

TABLE OF CONTENTS.

I

Table of Contents   xiii

II.

Table of Contents

APPENDICES.

BEHIND AND BEFORE

§ I

THAT the possible relations of Statesmanship to the study of History form an interesting subject of speculation, has long been admitted. Recent events—the great War and its sequel—have given to this admission a practical and painful bearing. In making a fresh attempt to discuss the questions involved in the subject it is unnecessary to apologize therefor otherwise than by confessing a sense of one's own insufficiency. From time to time in these latter years many a student must have felt troubled by serious doubts when noting strange and significant turns of public policy. He must again and again have wondered whether measures full of grave consequence had been adopted (often suddenly) with sound knowledge of the conditions existing in each particular case. He must have reflected that the conditions arising from present circumstances, closely connected with the past, would in most cases be extremely complex. This complexity, very evident to a student aware of the limitations of his own knowledge,—was it equally clear to public men working under great pressure[1], instructed mainly by the officials of the hour, and, however able and willing to learn, lacking the leisure to digest? As time went by, and various steps taken had to be retraced, he would more surely detect evidence of unhappy miscalculation in public policy. That the

---

[1] This situation is well illustrated in the earlier chapters of Mr Winston Churchill's book, *The World Crisis*.

psychology[1] of peoples, their circumstances, their resources, their traditions, had been misunderstood or even ignored, would appear probable, in some cases certain: and he would be tempted, rightly or wrongly, to censure the action of Government as ill advised from lack of knowledge. But he might also reflect that, if the Government erred from lack of the equipment needed for duly appraising circumstances (that is, from inadequate knowledge of the past), so too might his own judgment[2] be at fault for lack of a full knowledge of the present. The latest and perhaps the most convincing details would not be at a private critic's disposal.

But when all is said and done, and full allowance made for the difficulties besetting alike action and criticism, there still remains a feeling that in public policy, as in other departments of human affairs, some relation must exist[3] between study and decision. Hence it comes that men have for centuries been groping their way towards ascertaining what this relation really amounts to. That is, how far and by what methods the present generation can guide its action for the benefit of the future by a just appreciation of the past. This striving has expressed itself in many ways, more particularly in dogmatic assertions superficially attractive. That history repeats itself, that

[1] See the striking criticisms of G Le Bon, *The world in revolt* (Eng trans 1921).

[2] I venture to illustrate this from my own experience. Eager search for information as to the condition of foreign countries had led me to right conclusions in most cases, but as to Russia I found myself quite wrong.

[3] See Appendix E, *Knowledge and Action*.

it is philosophy teaching by examples, that nations (or bodies politic) have their course of growth and decay like human beings (or bodies natural), and that this analogy offers a sound basis for reasoned conclusions, are specimens of these dogmas. Facts can be cited in apparent confirmation of such views, and the ordinary citizen subjects them to no more rigid scrutiny: thus they become current and insensibly take possession of the popular mind. This prepossession shews itself in many ways; for instance in the demand for more 'history-teaching' in schools. This rests on a notion that the mere acquisition of historical facts has a value independent of their correlation and interpretation. A fairly-educated and sensible man once said to me that by History he understood the bare narrative of events in the order of their occurrence; all the rest was mere opinion of this or that historian, for which he had no use. In short, give him a chronological record, and he could and would draw his own conclusions. I have detected the same notion at the back of the minds of many other men, and am convinced that it is widespread.

Now, would the ordinary citizen apply this principle to matters within the scope of his own trade or profession? Surely not. To verify details, to appraise their importance both severally and in correlation, to estimate successfully the probable influence of external facts on internal working, are qualifications vitally necessary for successful management, and he knows that their presence is what distinguishes the professional from the amateur. Though no Socrates, he knows when he really does know

anything and when he does not. Of his own capacity, as
of other men's, he is a severe judge. Thus a famous
'crammer' some years ago, finding that pupils were
failing in the particular subject which he himself taught,
dismissed himself as he would dismiss an incompetent
assistant, and engaged a competent assistant to remedy
his own defects. This was 'business,' that is, commonsense. I pass on to consider what are the aims of studies
in general, be their subject matter what it may. Thus
I hope to make clear the bearing and limits of my
argument.

The general aims of study may be classified under
three heads: (a) the making of specialists capable of
extending and deepening this or that study, (b) the
simple gratification of human curiosity, (c) the increase
of human competence[1]. It is with this last that I am
here concerned. But they all overlap each other to some
extent: in practice we can only treat each by itself provisionally, according to our point of view at the time.

Let me take concrete examples, such as Physiology
and Engineering. The practising Doctor or Engineer
applies the results of study directly to professional
problems that call for solution. If his attempt at solution
fails, it follows that either the results of study need correction, or the problem has not been rightly conceived.
If it is the special science that is at fault, further study
is needed to bring its results nearer to the perfect certainty after which science strains, and so to render it a

[1] Of the last, the preparation for examinations as a means of
personal advancement may be regarded as a commercial satellite.

more trustworthy instrument for the uses of professional art. If the error is one of diagnosis, then evidently some element or elements in the problem have been overlooked or not sufficiently appraised. But if the results of study are sound, and the problem rightly conceived, the solution offered is bound to be successful. It is true that diagnosis may be vitiated by ignorance of important details which the professional man could not have before him at the critical moment. Facts may be inadvertently or deliberately concealed, and the patient may die or the bridge collapse prematurely. Practical action in a given case at a given time is ever exposed to accidents. But errors thus occasioned do not invalidate the scientific conclusion; they only illustrate the pitfalls of professional art.

In short, so long as you are dealing with subject matter the condition and behaviour of which can be ascertained, your science is really science, and its conclusions can be successfully applied in the art and practice of a profession, occasional accidents, due to human weakness, notwithstanding. Accidents generally arouse further inquiry, and their lessons tend to promote further ascertainment of causes. And, the more perfectly this is achieved by science, the more assured efficiency is given to art, concerned with effects. But let us suppose the existence of a subject matter less material and more elusive in character, in dealing with which it is not possible to ascertain the relation of causes and effects with scientific accuracy. In such a case the results of study will surely be more or less provisional. A con-

clusion will imply the unexpressed reservation 'that is,
provided no other cause has been overlooked or is still
unknown.' And if for any reason the practical art that
should apply these provisional results must all the time
necessarily continue in function, it must surely be unable
to apply them with confidence and firmness. For, if
doubt arises, and the study is renewed and a higher degree
of certainty thereby attained, there has still been a lapse
of time. Hence the problems with which the art has to
grapple are likely to be no longer quite the same as they
were at the moment when a renewal of study was seen
to be required.

Now in the case of History, taken as the study of
past generations of men in association, the difficulties
arising from the nature of its subject matter cannot be
ignored. To tell us that History is past Politics and
Politics present History does not help us much. We can
hardly say that at the present stage of mankind's career
History has reached a static condition; in short that there
exists an authorized[1] version of the doings and fortunes
of associated Humanity. We know that no such version
exists of the life-story of any people or nation, let alone
the human race. The history of even so articulate a
people as the Greeks remains a subject of research and
active debate. In so far as History is past Politics, it is
Politics in which causes and motives antecedent to
effects and actions can seldom be determined with the
moral certainty practically equivalent to proof. For the

[1] In the *Times* of 12–23 Jan 1922 there was a significant controversy under the heading *History to Order*.

records from which History works can never be war-
ranted to reach such a standard of completeness. Therefore its conclusions must be more or less provisional
verdicts. It cannot in any imaginable future attain the
status of an exact science.

And yet Politics, taken as the conduct of affairs of
associated men, must be continuously in function. So
far as it is an art, it operates in the choice of action.
Looking from the present to the future, it seeks the
desirable within the range of the possible; and the
possible is mainly conditioned by the results of the past,
which it is the task of History to ascertain. But Politics,
as a practical art, works under strict limitations of circumstance; above all, under conditions of time. For
things are ever moving on, and to dally is generally to
be out of date. History may reverse its verdicts at leisure.
Politics cannot undo an act or annul its consequences:
reversal of policy does not restore the precedent situation
unimpaired. If then Politics as an art depends on some
science for its principles, and that science is not exact,
the principles thence derived must be more or less
elastic. This position seems to be illustrated in the relations between Economics and Political Economy. The
rigid theory of the former may be as scientific and un-
answerable as you please in ideal circumstances. To buy
at the lowest price and sell at the highest is no doubt the
way to immediate profit. But the fact remains that low
first-cost may carry with it incidental disadvantages
enough to outweigh the advantages of high immediate
profit. In other words, the indirect gain attached to

acceptance of a higher scale of first-cost may render an apparently uneconomic bargain cheaper in the end. This truth is commonly recognized in the transactions of individuals; in those of states it is liable to be obscured by the recriminations of political partisans. So Political Economy, travelling by the road of Economic History, tends to allow a certain elasticity of practice and to become less doctrinaire in character than it was in its earlier days.

To return to Politics. In the continuous exercise of this art moments occur when a decision (that is, action) must be taken without leisure to reconsider principles, and to determine how far and in what respects they may need to be modified for present application. The capacity of doing this in strictly limited time is a function of what we call 'commonsense,' which expresses itself in happy improvisation[1]. And this capacity exists in very various degrees in various persons. Hence the great importance of personalities; for policies, to whatever causes they may be ultimately due, take effect through the agency of persons. This has always been so, though the partisan corruption of historical record may obscure the influence and responsibility of one statesman and exaggerate those of another. Therefore, while History cannot ignore the influence of individuals on the course of events in the past, it is most necessary to bear in mind that to attempt the judgment of personalities[2] is a task beset with infinite opportunities of error. Not only is the judge fallible

[1] Cf Lord Morley, *Notes on politics and history* (1913) p 58.
[2] See Appendix A.

himself; he probably has some unconscious bent or bias that he cannot detect or measure; but the record before him suffers from the same defect. Questions of motive are very likely to arise. At first sight it may seem that they are trivial. What matters is the act, not the motive that prompted it. But the motive is itself often a kind of indirect record of antecedent acts, and helps the inquirer to appraise the importance of those acts. When this is the case, motive is not trivial, and may be historically important.

Nor should we forget that persons (and through them policies) are liable to be pushed on or diverted or held back by sheer accidents. For instance, the removal or reappearance of an agent may inhibit or modify or revive action. And such accidents have not seldom happened. Historians cannot ignore them: their readers are perhaps liable to forget them. They come into consideration more particularly when a moral judgment[1] is attempted. Hence some would prefer to decline the censorial office altogether and to remain as non-moral as Macchiavelli. But this pose is a vain abdication. Sooner or later praise or blame, if not spoken, will be implied; and History, confined to a 'bone-dry' utterance, will become the mere confession of an insincere and unproven fatalism. This conflicts with a deep-rooted conviction at the back of men's minds. Their experience shews them that different actions have different results. Hence, whatever their religious creed, they feel that somewhere and somehow there is a distinction between

[1] See Appendix B.

right and wrong. They discern it in the present: why not in the past? Therefore, if History is to discharge a political duty in maturing the judgment of present citizens, it cannot dispense with a stimulant both harmless and wholesome, well suited to the constitution of men as they are.

That retrospective judgments of past actions and the policy of the agents may be erroneous, is manifest. But error of this kind is most mischievous when it leads a writer to misconceive the influences working at a given time, the conditions under which a statesman had to choose the direction of his policy. Take Pitt's Union scheme. The causes that drove him to carry out only a part of it are pretty well known. But his conduct on that occasion has been variously judged according to the various estimates of the comparative value of the influences under which his decision had to be made.

Another great and subtle danger lurks in the use of analogies[1] and parallels. On the face of it they sound well, and are apt to carry conviction to superficial observers. They seem at times to offer a satisfactory solution of some present problem to men who would like to see their way, but who have not the knowledge or leisure or will to test the comparison of past and present situations. It is not the historian himself that should be misled by such apparent resemblances. He will know very well that situations never recur so exactly as to furnish material for strict argument. But it is not easy to impress on readers or hearers the limitations and

[1] To this subject I return below.

reserves that enable the historian to employ such comparisons as mere passing illustrations and nothing more. The ordinary citizen (whose case I am here considering) is apt to take resemblances for actual parallels and thereby to be led into a jungle of fallacy. It is not by a treacherous process of facile assent that he can improve his capacity of judging the needs of the present with the help of a study of the past.

In seeking to indicate the difficulty of applying the lessons of History to the practical problems of Politics, two sources of error[1] vitiating judgment call for particular notice. One of these is the temptation to ignore or insufficiently to recognize the open or latent forces of tradition and circumstance that were operative at the moment under review. Thus in the above-cited case of Pitt we may make allowance, perhaps insufficient, for the power of the Crown in 1800, while overlooking the unofficial but significant fact that George III was on the whole popular. To multiply instances would be easy: the point is that judging the past requires a full appreciation of the silent influences as well as of those openly expressed. The converse error consists in the unintentionally misleading attitude sometimes adopted in relation to new influences. It is hard to discover exactly at what moment a new influence began to operate, comparatively easy to say when it was first recognized openly as a factor in political life. The historian is confronted with a task of peculiar delicacy. By laying undue stress on the visions of some isolated theorist, he may

[1] To these I return below.

easily antedate the working of a cause that a little later was undoubtedly operative: thus he will be guilty of anticipation. By assuming too readily that a cause undoubtedly operative later was in fact not working at a given earlier date, he may assign a disproportionate value to influences that were failing and almost spent. Thus he will blur the picture of a continuity which he would probably be the first to assert. Perhaps the movements of British fiscal policy down to the triumph of Free Trade in 1846 are a good instance of the difficulties here suggested. But the further you go backward in time, the greater in general is the difficulty; records on the whole are less complete, interpretation on the whole is more uncertain, in spite of some notable exceptions, and this largely because it is much easier to rediscover acts and institutions than to ascertain convincingly how they worked. That they once existed, may be proved: it is less easy to ascertain all the reasons why they failed.

Hence it follows that for the present purpose, the strengthening of a citizen's judgment in matters political, Ancient History is, of the three conventional divisions, less available than Medieval, still less so than Modern. The fall of 'ancient' civilization left a real gap in the story of human experience, dissemble it as you may. It left important survivals, but survivals only: the future lay with Medieval germs, mostly developing in the debris of Ancient decay. The notion of a world-empire died hard, leaving behind it the ideal of an universal religion, and its world was in effect confined to Europe. The ghost of the old Roman Empire haunted the scene, but the chief vital legacy of that Empire was the transformation of religion From a medley of local usages—racial, tribal, domestic,—a new principle had emerged in such strength that it spread beyond the Roman frontiers and gradually dominated the barbarian world. That all mankind were, or could be, on an equal footing in relation to the supernatural, was on the face of it a mighty unifying force. Was not the world with all its various peoples in a fair way to become one great unit of brotherhood, and the Roman Peace of subjection to be superseded by the Peace of Christ? Why this did not come about, is not for me to discuss: that it did not, is certain. But if unity was not achieved, our interest shifts to the inquiry—on what principles and by what means was the Medieval state-system built up? Historians of the Middle Ages must tell us of the growth of Feudalism, of its stubborn resistance to the encroachments of monarchs, a struggle not finally decided till quite Modern times, and of the social and economic movements that went on side by side. So far we have reached the establishment of Kingdoms, and (the Crusades notwithstanding) the bearing of policies and events is European.

Modern history really begins with gradual unsettlement of men's minds on points of religious creed or practice. This was closely connected with the revival of learning, but the soil was prepared by the spread of disgust at ecclesiastical abuses. Geographical discoveries and a new birth of natural science gave irresistible impetus to the forward movement destined to recast the ideas of men and to remodel their institutions in one department after another. In the political field, Europe gradually lost its monopoly of civilized interest. Intercourse between peoples increased. Monarchic governments were still the rule, and for a time they even tended to grow in scale and intensity. But popular rights were not wholly extinct in all countries, and the growth of large states, rendering direct participation of the people in their own government practically impossible, led to a political dilemma. Unconsciously, European men had either to submit to autocratic monarchs, or to devise and achieve some means of expressing their will[1] authoritatively by deputies. In England this meant the development of what had been achieved in the Middle Ages. But the normal solution (as in France and Spain) was the establishment of autocracy of a centralized military type. This form lasted long. Only in recent times have Representative systems slowly and sporadically prevailed: in most states they are a thing of yesterday, inspired by conscious and perhaps hasty imitation, assertions of freedom. No wonder that their operation sometimes suggests a comparison with delicate instruments in the hands of amateurs. The most potent influence promoting these bold and sanguine experiments is what we call Nationality[2], the claim of social units to combine in political union with other units to which they feel drawn by community of race (real or supposed), by economic interests, by tradition or exchange

[1] Appendix I refers to this point in connexion with the republican systems of Holland and Switzerland.
[2] See Appendix C.

of services, in short by any sympathy that draws them together and parts them from the rest of the world. For if Medieval movements produced Kingdoms, the Modern are (at present) producing Nations.

It seems undeniable that, if lessons are to be learnt from History as an equipment for practical Politics, it is in the experience of recent times that they must chiefly be sought. The further back you go, the greater is the difference between past and present conditions, and the effort to make due allowance consumes what the statesman must economize, invaluable time. On the other hand it may fairly be said that the comparatively near resemblance of more modern conditions may occasionally carry with it a danger of its own. The consultation of experience easily lapses into a search for precedents, and few processes are so liable to be misleading as this. The hope of finding a ready-made solution of a tiresome problem, and thereby reducing personal responsibility, tempts the human agent not to analyse differences with extreme severity. But the danger of precedent as compared with principle, well pointed out[1] by Mahan, is by no means confined to the sphere of naval affairs. And, so far as the ordinary citizen is concerned, it is a guide alluring in its simplicity and peculiarly fitted to lead his judgment astray. The mere suggestion of resemblance to some former situation, hastily thrown out in his newspaper, is enough to give a bent to his opinions and determine his vote. The busy or excited voter has not the time or temper for calm study of a

[1] Mahan, *Influence of sea power upon history*, pp 7, 9.

tangled issue. The position may perhaps be illustrated
by the history of the measures adopted during the nineteenth century with the aim of establishing peace and
prosperity in Ireland. Again and again it was argued
that this or that concession[1] would produce the desired
result: what had been remedial in Great Britain would
surely effect a cure in Ireland. But vainly the British
voter yielded to apparently cogent arguments. For the
eminent leaders were in truth blind guides leading blind
followers to the ditch. Their arguments were a series
of fallacies: either supposed precedents were worthless,
or the remedies, once possibly effective, were applied
too late. So, with the very best intentions, we have
landed ourselves in the present pass.

In the preceding paragraphs I have dwelt somewhat
fully on certain sources of political error, because I hold
them to be of peculiar importance in the politics of my
own country. Great Britain has lost the checks on hasty
legislation that once formed part of her constitution.
And she has not as yet created any new ones, such for
instance as have been found useful in the United States.
Many good citizens view with uneasiness or alarm the
unquestionable fact that a passing wave of delusion
may sweep us into a position of grave embarrassment.
A measure may be carried in haste, perhaps involving
consequences which the mass of the citizens neither
intended nor foresaw. Even if repealed at once, the fact
of its enactment must have evil effects; at the very least
it will shake public confidence in the Legislature. Kept

[1] See Appendix D.

in force, it will provoke evasion and discontent, being unsustained by any belief in its moral obligation. Now, when all is left to depend on the hurried action of impatient partisans, and yet no act is consummated without consequences, all depends on the judgment of fallible men exercised at a particular moment. On what can we rely to insure so far as possible that this judgment (I assume it honest) shall be sound? What security is there now for the normal prevalence of a calm and thoughtful policy, other than knowledge and wisdom in the masses and (more particularly) in the leaders of the passing hour?

And this, in some form or other, means education as a means of increasing the competence[1] of citizens. The next step then is to consider the possibilities of education as a practical means to the end in view. On its advantages it is needless to dwell: they are generally admitted. But that it also has its own dangers is not always candidly confessed. I will treat it as a qualifying condition in three grades distinguished by a lower or higher standard of thoroughness. The citizen who can barely read and write is obviously a person dependent on others for the information which reaches him coloured by the party prepossessions and interests of others. He does not understand the things reported, and has no suspicion of the manifold issues involved in them. He is just a vote and no more; unhappily there are many voters of the kind.

---

[1] 'In proportion as the structure of a government gives force to public opinion, it is essential that public opinion should be enlightened.' G Washington.

But the man of shallow mechanical one-sided[1] education (and this class is the most numerous of all) is not very much better off. True, he will probably get more information and grasp it more intelligently. Yet it is also true that such an education is sometimes a check upon honest readiness to learn. Learning implies testing, and a citizen of this type is mostly content to hear, or at least to believe, one version only. He is not 'uneducated,' and often quite unconscious of his own defects of equipment. And that recent attempts to supply a training in so-called 'civics' are wholly free from partisan taint[2] is more than I venture to affirm. The political importance of this class consists largely in the fact that popular leaders not seldom proceed from its ranks. The men of wider and more thorough education, comparatively few in number, are immensely valuable as a class, being more used to hearing both sides of a question fully stated, and aware of the pitfalls of judging from evidence often unavoidably incomplete. But such a man is no more exempt from human weakness than other men. The term of man's life is short, yet he cannot escape the necessity of dealing with issues proposed to him by his own past, and certain to involve consequences affecting for good or for evil the future of his kind. It matters not whether he openly bears a part in action or veils his responsibility under cover of judicious

[1] Cf Sir C P Lucas, *Greater Rome and Greater Britain* (1912) p 127, Hearnshaw, *Democracy at the Crossways* (1918) p 432.

[2] Written in 1922. It is to be hoped that the new Stott College will be above all suspicion. The opening speech of Mr Baldwin (*Times* 28 Sept 1923) certainly contained some excellent advice.

abstention. The conditions of human being are such that to abstain from acting is a significant form of action.

If then attention to the past and evaluation of its lessons are allowed to be a help in the citizen's discharge of an evident duty, and the study of history the most obvious means of getting this help,—how can we be afraid of having too much of a good thing? It is just at this point that considerations of the limits of human life and human faculty come in. All that the ablest and most industrious of men can absorb[1] in an average lifetime is but a part, perhaps but a small part, of the revealed history of the past from which the present is derived. Much has not yet been revealed; much never will be. It is possible, and very desirable, that his studies may have the pure effect of training his judgment, and thus develope in him political capacity of a high order. But it is possible too and undesirable, that they may increase his erudition out of proportion to his digestive power, and thus clog his judgment with insidious pedantry. Now, if statesmanship and good citizenship be the right practice of the political art, we must here note a danger; for pedantry is the very Judas of art. What we need is that our statesman and our good citizen, each in their several degrees, shall realize (and ever bear in mind) the infinite variety of circumstances,

---

[1] A letter in the *Times* of 18 May 1923, correcting the erroneous statement of a leading statesman on a point of historical fact, is a good recent illustration, taken together with the replies on May 22, 23, 25.

and the relativity[1] of opinions and policy, both past and present. If historical study furnishes them with this equipment, it will surely help them toward a cool and sound judgment of issues as they arise. For convenience sake the desirable condition of mind thus produced may be labelled Orientation.

Orientation[2] is valuable as a means of freeing the mind from the tendency to hasty deductions. Resemblances of past and present situations will receive careful thought from a man so qualified, but they will not mislead him. And this is a great gain. At the moment when a states-man has to be girding himself for prompt action, he has not the leisure to carry on research. He is almost con-fined to the official or unofficial information of the present hour. And only a well-orientated mind can weigh and use that information with cool intelligence. For instance, he cannot thoroughly read up the history of the Eastern Question or Ireland. But he can be conscious of the imperfection of his own knowledge (and that of others) and resist the temptation to adopt in haste the proposed measures of illusive temporary relief. He will not need to be told that bold and thoroughgoing measures sometimes cause less disturbance than piece-meal palliatives, while at other times procedure by small instalments works better. To which of these alternatives

[1] See Appendix G, and the remarks of E Jenks, *Walpole* (1894) pp 38–9, on the duty of a statesman to promote the growth of enlightened and sober political character.

[2] By this I mean the extension of practical capacity, largely empirical, however scientific its basis may be. It finds analogy in the professional skill of sailors, physicians, etc.

An aid to judgment 21

the realities of the present situation point, is for him to decide. That the decision arrived at may be carried out in good faith and with a minimum of friction, he must secure the support of his followers, a support as intelligent and whole-hearted as his powers of exposition can rally. That a popular leader, fully convinced of his own good intentions and his own sufficient knowledge, may by personal magnetism draw the multitude into ways that end in waste of energy without good result, we know by sad experience. To study much, and yet to miss the permanent and vital factors of the problem in hand, is a terrible thing when it happens to be the case of a politician at the height of his power; as we have learnt in our dealings with Ireland and the East.

That a man in face of grave responsibilities such as I have sketched above will desire to have at command knowledge in the light of which he may review official information, is likely enough. He will not wish to be the mere echo of observers who, however competent, have each his own special preoccupations and prejudices, and probably a less wide grasp of the general situation than he has himself. This is particularly the case in issues of foreign[1] policy. But in a time of crisis he will not be able to do much beyond discursive reading. In intervals of comparative quiet the aims of his study may easily be distracted by the capricious movement of events; he cannot be sure which of many impending issues will first call for his undivided attention. Desultory reading,

[1] See the remarks of E Scott, *Men and thought in modern history* (1920) p 87, on the recent talk of 'democratic control.'

aided by personal inquiry when chance offers, is likely to be his chief resource in the way of unofficial equipment, so long as he is bearing the burdens of office. Now, if we admit that in a statesman an ill-informed self-sufficiency may provoke disaster, while cramping pedantry may miss opportunities, how far can such an equipment serve to keep him in a clear and prudent course between these perilous extremes? I suggest that even an imperfect and discursive study under conditions of modern public life (that is, of time-pressure) may give useful and effectual help. But this only when conducted by a mind properly trained to disengage[1] facts of permanent significance from the medley of transient phenomena; that is, to extract genuine lessons, not mere material for party cries. To repeat a remark made above, it may be useful to seek a principle: it is a mischievous waste of time to seek a precedent. So too with the ordinary citizen. For him, in his kind and degree, that which is good for his leaders is good also.

To anyone who from academic surroundings considers the problem with which I am trying to deal the question at once occurs, how can student-courses be so organized as to aid in a practical solution? We know that proficiency is tested by examinations, and that the immediate aim of students is to prepare for these examinations. But we indulge a pious hope that a sound intellectual training is forwarded by the process. At the same time we feel a little uneasy lest it may tend to encourage the crude reproduction on

[1] Word borrowed from Lecky, *preface to history* (1878).

paper of matters industriously taught and mechanically learnt. By way of counteracting the risk of unintelligent 'cram,' we include under 'history' various theoretical studies, such as Economics and Political Science, and invite students to display their powers of thought and expression in Essays. So far as it goes, this is an excellent precaution. Whether it is sufficient to insure the healthy digestion of the strictly 'historical' subjects, the events and movements of the past, is not so clear. It seems rather analogous to a tonic than to a specific remedy. The danger that masses of detailed history may, if not speedily forgotten, become a burden[1] of ill-digested matter, a lifelong predisposition to pedantry, does not seem to be met. And, if success in examination be not the sole aim of study, if the formation of habits of judgment that will continue to function in later life be a worthy object, the danger here suggested cannot be dismissed as trivial. Surely we do not wish to equip our young citizen with a mass of historical lumber, dead stuff on which dust will be settling ever more thickly in the course of years.

If we start from the system of teaching by lecture with an examination-test in prospect, and our aim be to train a considerable number of citizens in the exercise of judgment on public affairs, we need to guard against a danger that besets this system from the first. Examinations tend to become agencies for recording degrees of 'merit.' Competition serves as a stimulus to industry. In order to ascertain the merits of the ablest students,

[1] Cf Bishop Stubbs, *Lectures* pp 18–9.

the range of the subjects in which the test is applied tends to exceed the receptive and digestive capacity of the average student. Is there not a danger that he may be overladen in the attempt to cope with a mass of material beyond his powers? If so, what is the chance of his gaining what I have called orientation, the sound basis of judgment in his later years of civic life? The same kind of question may be asked no doubt in connexion with other subjects; for a training that for the ablest students is reasonably exhaustive may for the average student be unreasonably exhausting. That is, it may impair elasticity of mind and enfeeble thought. But historical study is commonly supposed to contribute a special equipment fitting a citizen to bear an enlightened part in politics. Therefore in connexion with this subject the question has a special significance. And my conclusion is that, for the purpose of which I am now speaking, it is important that the material through which the average student is conducted should not be excessive in bulk. It is more desirable that he should follow his subject with lively interest, and should not be bewildered by too wide a range of topics, than that he should be driven to mechanical acquisition of facts, however interesting in themselves those facts may be. If a young man is to gain a genuine equipment for his later civic life, his student career should leave him not stale but fresh.

When I speak of matters as interesting, it may be well to distinguish between two kinds of interest. There is that which I may label Antiquarian. This may provide

valuable training in a region remote from latter-day
passions and problems, more particularly in ages before
Christianity introduced the burning questions involved
in the position of the Church. But this interest, however deeply felt, is mainly cultural. There is also that
which I may call Relative. This also may provide
valuable training, but it has a further value as being
to a greater or less extent in touch with present passions
and problems: that is, as admitting cautious comparisons
(of course not true analogies) between present and past,
and therefore not unfruitful even for the practical statesman. Now the former of these is an interest wholesome
for the young student as exercising his talents on a comparatively passionless material. He is not likely to be
Whig or Tory in dealing with the history of Rome. So
far well; but his interest in (say) Roman history, unless
followed by an equal interest in the history of later ages,
will not carry him far in the way of maturing his judgment as a citizen of his own country in the present
age. The world around him is strewn with wreckage
of a post-Roman past, relics of growth and decay,
stagnations and upheavals. Beliefs that once dominated
millions, and led them unquestioning to acts of enormous
consequence, are dead or dying. The map of the world
is in itself a sufficient proof that in study of ancient
conditions little or no practical suggestions for modern
policy are to be found. Not only have discoveries East
and West, and the expansion of European stocks, en-
larged the area to be kept in view by statesmen. In
Europe itself the whole scene has been changed by the

emergence of national[1] consciousness and the amazing growth of nations. In the view of Polybius, the ruling tendency was towards absorption in the dominant Roman unit. In our day the insistent claim is that of Nationality: that is, the establishment of independent units based on actual popular sympathy, whatever be the interests or sentiments from which such sympathies arise.

And here we come upon a situation full of grave difficulties, puzzling not only to the statesmen of new nations but to those of friendly nations desiring to guide their own policy wisely. A generous impulse to lend a helping hand to struggling peoples, endeavouring to consolidate national states, may, if misdirected, do more harm than good. Recent experience plainly illustrates this truth. It is to be hoped that our own country at least has learnt the significant lesson. For the number of these new national states is now considerable, and may offer many opportunities of error. Our statesmen need constantly to bear in mind the simple fact clearly exemplified in the history of the modern past, that nationality in aspiration and nationality in function are two very different things.

In the stage of aspiration the force of nationality moves simply and easily, conscious of no restraint or check other than a hated external control. This extra-national control the 'national' groups or sections readily combine to remove. But, once installed in function, the 'national' forces have to face problems hitherto dimly recognized, if at all. Their common security rests on

[1] See Appendix C.

development of solidarity; that is, on their firm establishment as a nation. But in the attempt to effect this they are hindered by the difficulties that can no longer be ignored. For instance, there is sure to be some conflict or rivalry of material interests. It is not easy to point to a national territory in which the immediate interests of all sections are so far identical as to smooth the path of national finance. They do diverge, and to reconcile them consistently with a sound financial system is no easy task, for each section fancies that it is being made to bear an undue share of the common burdens. From such feelings jealousies arise. There are however ties of kindred blood and tradition which might be expected to assuage animosities and prevent the evil effects of jealousy. But experience teaches that these ties are not always as operative as they promised to be. Minor local differences[1] of custom and sentiment are not extinct, and in the variety of material interests these differences are apt to revive with new strength. External control being removed, and deferred hopes now apparently realized, the consciousness of unsurmounted obstacles still remaining in the form of their own divisions is a disappointment to patriotic citizens. The result too often is that the lurking antipathies of kinsmen are turned upon each other, and even issue in ruinous party strife. Nor is this matter for wonder. The liberation of a 'national' unit necessarily implies self-government under a very 'free' constitution; and the new nation undertakes

[1] The result of the March 1923 elections in Jugo-Slavia, a victory of racial groups, is a recent illustration of this.

the hardest of tasks without the gradual training of practical experience. A tyrannous majority may conduct the state to ruin: a noisy and restless minority may thwart the achievement of national cohesion. The situation is one in which a Carlylese hero may find scope for his energies, but the chances of failure are surely greater than those of success.

I trust I have not overdrawn this picture of normal difficulties that embarrass the statesmen and citizens of new national states. Now, if this were all, if the newly established governments were assured of a quiet time in which to work out their own destinies undisturbed, it would be the obvious duty of their well-wishers to let them alone. But recent events prove that in some cases no such respite can be relied on. If a new state is menaced or attacked by a neighbouring power or powers, what should a friendly power do? This is a question to which there is no plain general answer. Each case has its own peculiar perplexities. In dealing with it much curious knowledge may be helpful, and the past record of several powers may need to be carefully considered in coming to a conclusion on the case of one. That this is so, may be clearly seen if we take such cases as Finland or Poland. Without some knowledge of the histories of Sweden, Prussia, Russia, not to mention Austria, Turkey and France, consideration of such cases would probably end in mistaken conclusions. Turn to the Balkan countries, and this truth stares you in the face. A statesman who has to find a policy applicable in dealings with that part of the world should be leniently judged. In such a patch-work mosaic of races, religions, customs, traditions, it is no easy matter to go right. But a knowledge of the main facts in the historic past is worth something, at all events better than the 'cooked' statistics published in support of racial or religious claims.

Perhaps I have said enough to indicate the danger that may arise from ill-considered policy in cases like those to which I refer, and the way in which knowledge of the past may help to inspire caution and a better understanding of situations. History may also serve to remind statesmen that in modern times states have become more linked together by community of economic interests, owing to expansion of international commerce. Unwise action abroad reacts at home to an extent formerly unknown: if a leader involves his country in a definite policy towards another state or states, his own country will in a greater or less degree feel the effects of that policy for good or evil. To miss this truth is to be blind to the lessons of modern history; and the statesman who errs thus exposes himself to rude punishment at the hands of popular discontent. A blunder may be recalled, but it remains as an awkward and probably mischievous fact. At the very least there has been a sad waste of time and energy.

In the attempt to turn historical study to account as a means of strengthening political judgment it is necessary to guard against certain evident dangers, the chief of which are those of slovenly comparison. In the region of fact there is false analogy, the deceptive equation of different things. Closely connected with this is the chronological fallacy, the equation of things similar when taken by themselves but different in significance and value through the difference of the respective times of their occurrence. The latter error shews itself in two clearly marked forms. We may so antedate a cause as to make it appear operative before it really was so, attributing to it effects that were really due to some other cause or causes. An error of this kind—call it Anticipation—is obviously fatal to sound judgment. The converse error is Protraction, which is an inclination to postdate a cause, making it appear operative after it has really ceased to be effective. And between these extremes there are of course endless opportunities of error varying in degree. The historian may unwittingly be guilty of such lapses under the bias to which human nature often yields, and perhaps at times be shaken by alternating gaps and plethora of evidence not easily interpreted. He must wrestle with his difficulties as best he may. The ordinary reader is apt to be unconsciously misled by a much simpler but not less treacherous influence, that of conventional metaphor[1]. Subtly entwined in common speech, these figurative expressions are not merely the ornaments of rhetoric. They tend to create a false background, on which events appear in unreal sequence and relation: and this to a greater extent than one is *a priori* disposed to believe. Four of these metaphors are so commonly in use that they may be named here without irrelevance. *Nautical*—the ship of state and its

[1] See a very interesting passage in Coulton, *Five centuries of Religion* (1923) p 140, on growth of the power of metaphor.

navigation. *Medical*—the state as patient and its doctors. *Botanical*—the state as plant and its cultivators. Widest of all, and now much in vogue, the *Biological*—the state as a living organism, subject to conditions strictly analogous to those of all animated being, and its phenomena interpreted (and possibly controlled to some extent) by the principles of the great and growing Science of Life.

Now, if current language not only records current ideas but helps to popularize the corresponding points of view (and this I think it does), these applications of metaphor are not insignificant. A number of persons, not citizens of the most ignorant and heedless class, are watching the trend of contemporary events, and even devising remedies for contemporary evils; but their points of view and their several mental attitudes are not identical. Some are more concerned with the immediate future, wishing to remove manifest obstacles and relieve the state from embarrassments that hinder wholesome progress. To others it appears that a conscious and constant attention is and always will be required to keep the forces of the state in healthy function. Others again hold that the present social and economic system is moving surely towards disaster, and call for its complete reconstruction as the only means by which Civilization, the achievement of mankind's immemorial struggle, can be saved. These are very different views: and those who hold them are not likely to be in close agreement as interpreters[1] of the past. To past experience they will

[1] See a letter of Mr G M Trevelyan in the *Times Lit Supp* 30 March 1922.

sooner or later be found appealing. Each school will provide its own interpretation; and interpretation sooner or later reacts upon narrative. There is therefore a not negligible danger that published histories, to which readers resort for instruction, may be infected by this or that bias, without any deliberate untruthfulness on the part of their authors. That there have been, and probably will yet be, instances[1] of this failing, can hardly be denied. All the more then is it necessary that, as I have implied above, the reader who reads to strengthen his political judgment should know how to read. And this is just the very equipment that sound academical teaching[2] is above all things called to supply.

To employ a convenient simile, the man who studies history with the aim of strengthening his political judgment resembles the navigator voyaging in imperfectly charted seas. He must ever be on the alert to detect rocks and shoals and to make allowance for currents the exact set and laws of which are not as yet thoroughly known. A good instance of the perplexities that will surely trouble him is the old question of moral judgment[3] in issues of the past. Can questions of right and wrong be fairly treated long after the circumstances in relation to which they arise have passed away? Should they be regarded abstractedly as issues referable to, and determinable by, ethical rules accepted at the present time of judging? Or should it be the first business to

---

[1] The stock instances are Macaulay and Grote.
[2] See Appendix H.
[3] See above p 9 and Appendix B.

Moral judgments 33

ascertain the rules accepted at the time when this or
that policy was adopted, and to judge it solely by its
conformity to those rules or violation of them? Further,
is the historian bound to pass any moral judgment at
all? Is it his duty to do so? And the reader, will he in
fact gain anything by it? That he is not unlikely to
imbibe a prejudice, will perhaps be admitted. But this
is not all. A derived prejudice may easily take a more
definite form in the reader's mind than in that of the
writer, and the habit of viewing things under the
influence of a certain bias may soon harden the original
prejudice until it becomes permanently misleading.
Accordingly there are grave authorities[1] who would
exclude moral judgments from histories altogether:
while others, convinced that human affairs cannot be
profitably discussed without considerations of right and
wrong, take a different[2] view, and believe it a good thing
to maintain a sort of standing tribunal of public opinion,
before which issues of the kind are exposed to a con-
tinual process of disentanglement and revision by competent advocates in learned debate.

Perhaps no better specimen of such issues can be
found than the still wide differences of opinion evoked
in comparing the positions of Charles I and Cromwell,
their acts and aims, and in attempting a moral judgment
of their methods and motives. In this highly complicated

[1] See an interesting letter (1875) quoted in the Memoir of
W E H Lecky p 106.
[2] I think I may fairly cite the case of Lord Acton as representative of this view.

case, to stand aside in indifference, and form no opinion
at all, is humanly almost impossible. The political and
religious atmosphere of the time is so charged with
conflicting ideas and claims, and the fierce debate of
right and wrong (as then understood) is so inseparable
from moral considerations, that a student vainly strives
to keep clear of all partisan feeling. To take the main
issue as to the principles of authority and government,
we have on the one hand the monarchic idea, founded on
the past and with the Tudor tradition still fresh, but
out of date, and therefore unreal; on the other hand, the
new view of royal responsibility, at present crude and
premature, but real. To balance these claims is no simple
matter. And when they are brought into connexion with
the religious issues of the stormy seventeenth century it
becomes more and more difficult to reach an honest and
final judgment. When the characters of notable public
men are taken into account (which can hardly be
avoided), and the effect of personalities recognized, the
difficulty becomes extreme. The sincere historian is
driven to stifle praise and to blame with reserve, as we
see in the great work of S R Gardiner. But there is
another point of view, looking not to facts paraded in
public life but to evidence of economic wellbeing and
the comparative prosperity of various classes. Thorold
Rogers[1] draws attention to the improved position of
wage-earners under the Commonwealth, a very significant fact: and the prompt abolition of feudal services
at the Restoration in the interest of landowners is

[1] *Economic interpretation of History* (1888) pp 44, 287.

notorious. These and other details suffice to indicate an influence quietly at work throughout the period, which cannot be labelled as either political or religious, but was probably overlapping both and tending to intensify them.

Now in this subject, the seventeenth-century struggles referred to above, we surely have material which under judicious treatment may be of great educational value. It is not easy to find a period in which so many lessons of first rate importance are offered to a student, and offered in an indisputable form. The misjudgments of contemporaries as to the relative strength of existing influences are most instructive. Attempts to continue and extend principles of government already obsolete in Church and State are no more inevitable failures than measures of reform for which the time is not yet ripe. Things move on in disconcerting ebb and flow. The actors in the scene suffer endless disappointments. They achieve very little of their aims, and that perhaps by some unforeseen accident. Are we now, the student may ask, any less blind than men were in that age? Perhaps not, we may reply, but we may learn to be more watchfully on our guard against the delusions of hasty confidence, more fully aware that much of what we desire and foresee can only be the fruit of time.

For the modern student, looking back into a past period, is in a position to view it as a whole. He cannot help inquiring how the conditions of the period arose out of those in the preceding age. Nor can he miss the significance of those in the succeeding one, develop-

ments from that with which he is primarily concerned.
To take the instance cited. The confusing vicissitudes
of the seventeenth century are the transition from the
Reformation and Tudor Monarchy to Protestant Succession and the Hanoverians. Here is a momentous
change, brought about by a series of events, in which
the most striking are the Civil war and the political
Revolution of 1688. But these two events were themselves the result of many forces continually operating
in combination or conflict. The further the student
proceeds in disentangling and appraising these forces,
the less inclined will he be to wonder at the apparent
blindness of contemporaries. He will recognize that they
could not shake off the burden of inherited tradition,
however much sincere enthusiasts might wish to do so.
He will constantly remind himself that men of those
days, knowing nothing of the future, had no means of
guessing what methods and measures offered at this or
that moment the best prospect of promoting a desired
result. This remark may seem to be nothing more than
a platitude wrapped in verbiage. And such it is, no
doubt: but it is an attempt to illustrate by a concrete
instance the way in which historical study may for
statesman or citizen have a real educational value. For
the student will not study to much purpose, if he learns
to do justice in judging others, but omits to apply his
conclusions on their case to a clearer understanding of
his own.

In considering the possible service of History as a
helper and guide in the practice of Politics it may be

well to set out in order what are the questions implied in the attempt to get hints from the past. The inquirer, confronted with proposed measures from which certain results are expected, and probably also with assertions that action of the same kind has successfully been taken on a former occasion, seems driven to ask[1] the following questions, and to judge the proposals in the light of what he believes to be the true answers.

A. *Questions of past fact.*

(*a*) What exactly was done on the occasion cited?

(*b*) In what circumstances was it done?

(*c*) With what design?

(*d*) With what result?

B. *Comparative considerations.*

(*a'*) Can we do the same thing now?

(*b'*) Will present circumstances permit the same formal action to be the same in character?

(*c'*) Is our present design really the same as that of the actors on the occasion cited?

(*d'*) Can we reasonably expect the results of our action now to be the same as those of theirs then?

C. *Further cautionary considerations.*

(*a''*) Do we certainly know all that was done then, and what was merely contemplated?

---

[1] See Appendix H on the forward or backward methods of study.

(*b″*) Do we certainly know how far preexisting conditions were then more or less favourable to action than they are now?

(*c″*) Are we quite sure of the scope of our design now, any more than they were then?

(*d″*) Are we any more able now to guard against unforeseen consequences than they were then?

Whatever may be the answers to these questions, the inquirer will hardly escape the consciousness that the proposals, if carried out, will be a great experiment. It may also occur to him, and may give him some anxiety, that experiment with materials imperfectly known and sometimes uncontrollable must leave a great deal to chance. Further, he may well reflect that experiment in human affairs is seldom or never pure (that is, scientific, made for research), but either partly or wholly made as a temporary resort in order to avoid or defer a present difficulty. In other words, the appeal to History in such a case as I have suggested amounts to requesting a Science to furnish means for the practice of an Art: and, if the Science be not exact, the practice of the corresponding Art cannot be surefooted and final.

While speaking of experiments, and the risk that they may be in truth no more than temporary expedients, we must not omit to note the change brought about by developments of 'popular' government in modern times. The normal author of political experiments is no longer an Autocrat but a Minister representing with more or less fidelity what is supposed to be the opinion of a majority of the citizens. He rises and falls on the 'popular' tide, sometimes with startling suddenness. From this precarious position there arises a new danger, that a scheme devised in good faith (and perhaps wisely) may not be allowed a reasonable period of trial, but may be swept away in a hurry under some wave of reaction. Now no one deliberately wishes to deform the national record with wasteful wreckage; least of all, the Minister whose name will be associated with such futilities. No wonder then that Ministers, who can rely on being blamed for failure more generously than praised for success, often shew little forwardness to undertake responsibility. Men may be pardoned for not being in haste to start what they may not be allowed a fair chance[1] of carrying out; at the same time they probably feel bound to 'do something' in consequence of their own professions. In this dilemma they are apt to resort to compromise, as a means of committing their opponents to letting the measure have a fair trial. But compromise that disarms opposition is not unlikely to produce a measure undesirable on its own merits, and to effect little beyond some sharing of discredit between parties. A far deeper problem really underlies the danger I have here noticed. It is, how to ascertain the value of what passes for Public Opinion.

As history cannot, in consequence of the great change

[1] I am not forgetting that political leaders sometimes adopt and carry out the policy of their rivals, which they resisted when in Opposition. On the modern tendency to hasty and sweeping legislation there are some good remarks in E Jenks, *Walpole* (1894) pp 36–7.

referred to above, give much help in the consideration
of political experiments, so also its help in estimating
public opinion will be found small. For the modern
development of means of road and railway communications, of telegraphy and telephony, of cheap and copious
newspapers, has changed the situation enormously. The
difference in degree is so great as virtually to amount
to a difference in kind. Information, correct or incorrect,
no longer dribbles slowly from the centre to the counties
round; in a few minutes what is known in London is
known at Plymouth or Aberdeen. It comes in fragments:
assertion is often followed by correction or denial: but
it has the general effect of inviting simultaneous expression of opinion from all parts. Now there may be, and
probably are, issues on which the judgment of all sections
will be most genuine and valuable when expressed inde-
pendently and all at once. They may indicate the practical
limits of a possible policy. But their tenour may easily
be taken to mean more than it does mean. Local
influences at the moment may give them a more decided
character than a sound estimate of local opinion would
justify: and a judgment expressed in haste is less easily
revised at leisure. On the other hand there surely are
issues of importance on which it is better that opinion
should be formed slowly, and on which its simultaneous
expression is of no considerable advantage. Now the
most immediate expression of opinion comes from the
Press. We in Great Britain have reason to be thankful
that this powerful organ is so discreetly conducted as on
the whole it is. Worked in a downright bad spirit, it

might do incalculable harm. But it is a very modern power; how great that power is, we as yet hardly know. If I may venture to suggest that in some respects it is not always a safe guide, I would urge that newspapers are sometimes liable to do mischief by hasty recognition of 'mandates.' From a partisan point of view this is excusable, but in fact votes are never determined by simple considerations, and it is tempting not only to magnify but to misinterpret a party triumph.

For this matter of mandates is a source of endless confusion of thought. True, the return of a majority to Parliament does generally imply approval of the policy professed by the party to which that majority belongs. But the approval is mainly if not wholly given to the professed end or ends. Very seldom can it be taken as seriously applicable to the means, at least in detail: and it is over the means in detail that interests and opinions are most likely to diverge. When it comes to offering future gain at the price of present discomfort, human frailty and selfishness are apt to reassert their power without delay, and the moral force at the back of the Government dies down into simple reliance on the votes of their new majority. In a representative system worked by constituencies it may (and does) happen that this moral force is impaired by an automatic complication[1]. Seats are won by local majorities, some-

[1] In connexion with this it may be suggested that the defect here noted does not pass unobserved, and that its recognition tends to prevent apparent mandates from being taken too seriously. That devices for securing a more arithmetically exact representation of the total of voters would be an unmixed gain,

times large, sometimes very small. It may be (and sometimes is) the case that a majority of representatives is returned by a minority of the total of voters. Under such conditions the theory of a popular mandate halts somewhat lamely. What did the *vox populi* really mean? Political critics remind the public that in elections personal considerations often play an important part, and that accidental happenings shortly before polling-day are not unknown as disturbing influences. A few surprises at by-elections serve to increase the uncertainty. No wonder, if all this induces a creeping mistrust of the apparent stability of the Government.

But the situation I have sketched is not really so bad as it sounds in words. It is in truth inevitable, a result of the limitations of human capacity. There is no more searching test of the soundness of what we call our Civilization than the frank and loyal acceptance of the consequences of our own imperfection. Ingenious and well-meant schemes[1] have been devised in the endeavour to insure that expressions of the popular will shall be more final, or at least more exact. Of these, most notable is the so-called Referendum, which has been put in

is not hastily to be assumed. In the *Times* of 7 June 1923 is an account of an interesting proposal for securing that the majority in the country shall have a majority in the Chamber under the Italian constitution.

[1] The problems of Representation are ably discussed by Hearnshaw, *Democracy at the Crossways* (1918). See especially ch x *The rule of the Majority*. He distrusts mechanical nostrums. The elaborate machine system developed in the United States is described by R H Fuller, *Government by the People* (New York 1908), a disquieting story.

practice in Switzerland and in some of our own Colonies. This is in short the submission of a definitely drafted proposal, provisionally adopted by Parliament, to a popular mass-vote for approval or rejection. The citizens have a clear issue on which to vote Aye or No, and the poll settles the matter for the time being. Experience seems to shew that the plan chiefly operates in favour of an Opposition, negative forces being unusually alert on such occasions. But so far the initiative is assumed to rest with the existing government, whom defeat checks, but does not displace. There is however in Switzerland a further arrangement for inviting expression of the popular voice. If 50000 signatures can be procured to a proposal for new legislation, this constitutes a valid initiative, and a Referendum has in due course to be taken on the issue raised. On 3 Dec 1922 a case of this kind came up for settlement. A socialistic proposal, already rejected by the Parliament, but revived under this constitutional provision, was defeated[1] by nearly seven to one in a very heavy poll.

To work a Referendum[2] in a great populous state would surely be very difficult, and might lead to serious weakening of the fabric of government, which on a large scale is never too easily kept stable and in normally healthy function. So long as human qualities remain at about their present level, perhaps we need not expect

[1] On 3 June 1923 a bill for extension of liquor control was defeated by about 3 to 2. This was an ordinary Referendum.

[2] See J D Barnett, *The operation of the Initiative Referendum and Recall in Oregon* (1915). Readers of this book will perhaps shrink from favouring such devices.

or desire the general adoption of this expedient. The mass vote, as opposed to vote by constituencies, can hardly be suggested by anything in democracies of the ancient world. The doctrine, that direct personal assent on the part of the People is necessary to the validity of a legislative act, is the kernel of Rousseau's system, and it may be that Referendum is partly a child of the *Contrat social,* however much its application may be connected with the democratic traditions of Swiss cantons.

The other device, of polling in constituencies, but allowing the voter to record an alternative transferable vote—the so-called Proportional Representation—is an attempt to give at need some effect to 'second preferences'. Its strength is mathematical: its weakness lies, I think, mainly in the difficulty[1] of working so delicately calculated a scheme under the conditions of a secret ballot. Careful organization is required to see that it produces the result desired by party agents, who are already inclined to drynurse voters sufficiently. To extend the process to 'second' votes is a step further. The intelligent voter may prefer to keep thus much of his intentions to himself: the unintelligent may blunder in carrying out instructions. Personal relations to the candidates may in either case weaken a man's party orthodoxy, and many a voter will shrink from open confession of such considerations. These human details are not to be despised. Whether they can be eliminated by arith-

[1] The results of the Free State election in Ireland Sept 1923 seem to illustrate my point.

metical processes, and whether, if they could, it would be a real political gain, is beyond me to judge.

That inventions of this kind mark a gulf between the conditions of old and new politics, can hardly be denied. A common aim in both is the nervous striving to find some simple mechanism for ascertaining what passes for Public Opinion. They are evidence that observant minds have been shocked by the confused and capricious working of our traditional representative system. They imply a belief that a clearer and steadier expression of the popular will would inevitably conduce to better government. But this inference is not proven, perhaps not susceptible of proof. For as to the value of *vox populi* in itself, and not as a convenient means of gauging present possibilities, we are in the dark as much as ever. The political appliances may be improved (or at least altered), but the old stumbling-blocks remain; the frailty of human nature and the lapse of time. The voters may still misjudge their true interests: statesmen may still, when they come to act, be confronted with a situation different[1] from that with which they were appointed to deal. Surely this fact is a warning against the doctrine of 'mandates'. To be placed in office under a mandate vitiated by change of circumstances is a position worse than absurd; it is more than likely to be dangerous. If a policy other than that enjoined by mandate should turn out to be positively necessary, though carrying with it manifest evils, are the mandated

[1] Surely this was one of the most serious embarrassments of our own Parliament at the outbreak of the war in 1914.

majority in Parliament likely to be the best agents of that policy? It may reasonably be doubted. At such a juncture the majority may have to come to terms with the minority in opposition. And this arrangement, honourable to the patriotism of both sections, is (as we know) liable to develope into an uneasy coalition, in which the proper functions of a representative chamber are impaired. History supplies, I think, only one aid to criticism of such a situation. For there is a notable difference in this respect between the unreformed House of Commons and the present one. Members are nowadays more 'representative' than they were in (say) the life-and-death struggle with Napoleon. Perhaps they are better men; they are certainly less free to follow their own judgment. On the whole this may be a gain. But we must not look to secure the gain and avoid the drawbacks. Nor, in contrasting the efficiency of Cromwell with the inefficiency of the Stuarts, must we forget that Cromwell's government was the government of a minority.

In view of the now almost universal assumption of a democratic basis of government in civilized states, it may incidentally be asked, when and where do we find a genuine case of government by a majority? That is, by a majority of the citizens, not only possessed of constitutional power to control decisions by their votes, but actually and habitually exercising that power with effect. If the power merely exists in principle, and is seldom or never exerted in practice, can we speak of such a system as government by majority? In Repre-

sentation as worked by constituencies we have already
noted results by which the theory of majority-rule seems
to be stultified. And such results may recur in election
after election, for they are an inseparable accident of the
system. But it might be thought that under a non-
representative system, in which the citizen is himself a
legislator in person, no such result would occur. That
a direct system of this kind is only possible in small
states, is a point of no bearing in the present connexion.
Now I am not able to cite a single instance of direct
government in which it could be candidly affirmed that
the votes of an actual majority certainly and habitually
prevailed. Even in democratic Athens we hear of the
normal difficulty of securing full Assemblies, and of the
significant fact that it became necessary to provide a fee
for attendance. Yet even so the complaints of citizens'
indifference[1] and slackness are too definite to be ignored.
The provision of elaborate checks on legislative action
plainly confessed the truth that the Assembly was a
slovenly legislator, and could not be trusted to act discreetly in the general interest. Moreover at critical
moments, when wise decisions were of exceptional importance, it was nearly always the case that a large
percentage of citizens in their prime were absent on the
service of the state, not to mention those engaged abroad
in their private concerns. It therefore seems to me that
the majority of the Sovran People at Athens was seldom,

[1] The difficulty of keeping those present attentive to business
is graphically described in Demosthenes' speech on the Embassy
p 383 §§ 135–6.

if ever, in function at a given moment, and that their potential governing power seldom, if ever, became actual.

Now, to what general conclusion do these various considerations lead us? I can only state my own inferences, which are these. Wide extensions of the franchise are not to be blamed. While they appease discontent, they do not change the working of our institutions in any essential respect: they only enlarge the scale. But enlargement of the scale does tend to increase the difficulty of appraising the significance of elections. In course of time a regrouping of partisans may lessen the difficulty. But in a large civic body it will always be there; and the pernicious theory of mandates might become an intolerable evil. The poet's eye may foresee a time when 'the common sense of most shall hold a fretful realm in awe'. The statesman is tempted to add that, if it is to be effective, it must not lack adequate expression. And to this end the political projectors devise plans intended to make the expression complete, so that by improved machinery public opinion may be ascertained beyond a doubt. But, does this really solve the problem? Assume that it does so, for the moment of polling: the question raised above as to sudden change of circumstances (and therewith probably of opinion) is left unanswered: a mandate obsolete becomes for the representative a futility or a fetter. If duty compels him to disregard it, what was the good of it? If he feels bound to the letter of a pledge, what good can be expected from a government swayed by blind and vicious pedantry? Truth is, the desire of honest statesmanship is that the force of public opinion shall be not only ascertainable but also (and most of all) beneficial. This no machinery can insure. Human frailty admits liability to error, even in simple and quiet circumstances. It is therefore necessary that those who have to act in carrying out the popular will should have authority to interpret it at need according to circumstances. Frank recognition of this authority is, I repeat, the surest test of a great self-governing people's political maturity.

Whatever be any man's judgment as to the claim here put forth, the case is one well adapted to illustrate what I have said as to the possible value of historical study in political life. The surrenders of Walpole on the Excise question (1733) and on the war with Spain (1739) are instances of a great and prudent minister yielding to popular clamour, with results evil or doubtful, and at a time when representation was a farce. After 1832, when it was more of a reality, we find Peel casting aside his own record and deferring to popular sentiment under pressure of immediate necessities by (1846) repealing the Corn Laws. As to the ultimate results of his action, opinions may differ. That he had to bear imputations of treachery and the loss of political power, we know. But the thing had to be done, and posterity has taken a more kindly view of his moral courage. Now, neither of these cases is strictly parallel to the situation suggested above. The wider franchise and simultaneous polling have brought it about that the force to which it is necessary to bow, or which it may be a duty to disregard, is not extra-parliamentary agitation, but the pressure of a pledged parliamentary majority. The situation has no exact analogy to situations in the past. Yet I think that due consideration of crises in which policy had to be modified or reversed under the pressure of changed circumstances, cannot but be of use in training judgment. And between the duty of yielding to public opinion when it lacks regular means of expression, and of not following it unintelligently when it can and does express itself without let or hindrance, there is an inverted analogy. Sound judgment and moral courage are in both cases indispensable for arbitrating between rival principles and applying the decision in practice.

It will be seen that my argument leads to confessing the supreme importance of leadership. Nor do I shrink from glorifying that function. No observer of humanity will deny that mankind now need to be led as much as ever, or that wise leaders are few. Admitting the power of personality, few will deny that personal fitness may be developed by sound training. But a question may arise as to the comparative values of an education in general principles and a study of concrete facts in the history of the past. The former plan offers an alluring simplicity, but the necessity of making allowances and modifications in practice soon complicates its usefulness as a guide. It can supply apparently cogent reasons for doing or not doing this or that; but its doctrinaire tendency (not easily resisted) is a serious danger, when a policy has to be chosen at short notice, or in dealing with matters of which the public know little or nothing. A leader, who has gained a reputation in departments where he shewed himself a master, may mislead millions, and do no little harm, if he undertakes to solve problems that he does not understand[1] on principles that do not really fit the case. He may even bring to bear enough historical reading to impress the multitude and convince himself of the adequacy of his good intentions. Yet he may all the while be more hopelessly in the dark than many men of inferior gifts and less apparent knowledge. In the course of little more than fifty years we have seen the Irish question handled thus. Instead of finding out what Irish opinion and sentiment really wanted, and then deciding manfully to grant or refuse it, our statesmen never achieved a true diagnosis, but applied remedies for which we have had to pay dear and for which we shall never get any thanks. Perhaps a true diagnosis was not attainable: it was certainly not attained by misguided good intentions of British leaders. These men were not quacks in their own several lines; but their piecemeal concessions have only made the agony more prolonged and more ruinous, and amazed the world by a scene of unsurpassed tragic irony in real life.

If association, and in some degree cooperation, are allowed to be necessary conditions of what we call 'civilization' and 'progress', and if the further condition of leadership is no less necessary, it may be well to look a little deeper into these conditions. Joint action is not

---

[1] Lord E Fitzmaurice, *Life of Shelburne* III pp 527–9, blaming Pitt's belligerent policy in 1793, attributes it to his ignorance of foreign affairs, which made him the tool of Ministers of other countries. I cite this opinion merely to shew that I am not the first to note this particular danger.

peculiar to mankind, nor yet is leadership. Many other animals live and act in regular communities, and probably owe their survival in a 'state of nature' to the development of institutions favourable to their protection from others individually stronger. If so, this implies a faculty of memory, a capacity of learning to some extent by experience to avoid what is found to be harmful or even dangerous. That this is a memory for several particulars, not evolution of principles, was noted[1] by Aristotle, and surely he was right. So far, man and other animals travel side by side: indeed we might include all living things, down to the meanest weed that plagues the gardener. In the modern cant phrase, they are all 'out for power' in nature's fierce competition. But Man has a power that the others lack, namely the Power of Record. He does not depend on the memory of impressions made on individuals and effectively retained by some of them. The stone-cutter, the writer on various material sheets, the printer, mark stages in the development of his means of record. So the experience of earlier generations, more or less correctly represented, accumulates for the benefit of later. As time goes by, and mankind become more self-conscious, more aware of their own liability to error, they begin as citizens to do what they have been doing in the personal affairs of daily life; that is, to seek help in the judgment of public affairs from considering the successes and failures on record in their own past. At first they use this material very crudely, looking for direct examples and precedents, and

[1] Aristotle, *Ethics* VII 3 § 11.

the actual fruit of their inquiries is little or nothing of practical value. But sooner or later a more searching and appreciative criticism, gradually purging the records, exposing forgeries and falsehoods, and applying more scientific methods of comparison and interpretation, revives interest in the past. In other words, research supersedes rhetoric, and inquirers can tentatively feel their way to principles.

But, when this stage is reached, the difficulty of which I have spoken above is not long in making itself felt. As inquiry proceeds and numberless opinions and pre-possessions are found to require revision and correction, it comes home to inquirers how hard it is to attain final and exact conclusions. Evidence is too often scanty or conflicting. And, even when it suffices to make certain some particular fact, it does not always serve to make clear the bearing of that fact upon others. Disinterested students become convinced that study of the past must never lose sight of human nature, with all its limitations and vagaries, if it is to be a trusty helper in fortifying judgment. Now human nature is no simple factor in political problems, for which allowance can surely and easily be made. Full of elusive elements, the observers who appraise it with success are few, nor would they be able to give on demand a rational account of the grounds of their several estimates at given moments. The subtle sympathy, on which the soundness of their observation really depends, does not in the present state of knowledge lend itself to scientific explanation or compression in a formula. That it exists, and that it is far more efficient in some men than in others, is manifest; but you can hardly put it into words.

It is interesting to note that in some departments of life we habitually take account of human defects. For instance, Law and Medicine operate on this assumption, and it is a common footing of Religions. Yet all these do battle more or less successfully with the obscurity of the subject. We may ask, is there some characteristic of Politics that creates a special difficulty in that department? I think there is. I find it in the difference of approach, if I may so call it. The litigant and the patient (to take these instances) willingly or unwillingly resort to the practitioner, who deals with their controversies or complaints according to the methods of his art. The relation between the man of trained skill and the man who needs it is recognized in the professional fee. But in Politics, as understood and practised under any system of so-called self-government, it is the man who professedly offers the services of his presumed skill that invites the citizen to make trial of it. Hence the hackneyed pleasantry of comparing politicians to vendors of quack remedies, of course implying that their real aim is to advance their own interests. That a man is well qualified to take charge of the interests of the community, has generally at first to be taken on the authority of himself and a few supporters. Hence a new candidate is normally a strict party man, and a solid party backing is only to be had under the condition of definite pledges.

He then, who solicits the 'most sweet voices' of

voters, normally enters public life as a puppet[1] responding
to the strings pulled by party managers. Until he has
made his own force felt (which some never do), his own
fitness or unfitness for governmental duties is not tested.
He is a sort of servant taken on trial, qualifications and
all, and liable to dismissal; not an expert called in to deal
with critical issues. Nor is this arrangement a bad one
in practice, for the man is not an expert, and an apprentice-
ship is the simplest way of training him. Politics is not
a profession in the ordinary sense of the word. There is
no 'school', no examination to test formal qualifications.
It is only in an untechnical sense that we can call it
an Art: that there is no strict analogy between it and
the arts proper, was pointed out[2] by Aristotle. Yet-that
the process of acquiring 'virtues' (characteristic excel-
lences) advances on the same lines is admitted[3] by the
same inquirer. By doing our best imperfectly we at
length become able to do perfectly. But the difference
between strict operation by professional rules, dealing
with material of ascertained quality, and operation inevitably tentative throughout, limited by the capricious
phenomena of the human material, remains great. And
this everybody knows. It seems then that in the political
department we do recognize the existence of human
defects liable to impair the smooth and efficient working
of our institutions. Our language may at times dissemble

---

[1] The view of Sir H Maine, *Popular Government* (ed 1909)
p 30, on the power of wire-pullers seems to me too pessimistic.
[2] Aristotle, *Politics* III 16 § 6, cf II 8 § 24.
[3] Aristotle, *Ethics* II 1 § 4.

this recognition. In the course of a long life an observer will note many occasions on which great benefits have been absurdly expected from a mere change of Government. Through a series of expedients, devised by its imperfect and faltering agents, self-governing humanity gropes its way.

But at the present stage of the world's history we have much need to be on our guard against taking too narrow a view of what is implied in the notion of practical politics. There are influences which we are too apt to regard as not political at all, I mean the racial and hereditary. We are beginning to take account of these, but only beginning; interest in them is likely to grow steadily, if slowly at first. The tendency in inquiries into these questions must surely be to lay more stress on the quality of agents than on the value of political mechanism. If so, Politics will be brought more directly into touch with Natural Science, and will be engaged in attempting the solution of problems not to be solved by a majority of votes at some given date. Science will appeal to past history as well as to present observation. It may very well offer us a startling new interpretation of past facts and point to a new departure in self-government, based on recognition of truths ascertained by scientific research. Such a movement will amount to nothing less than a claim for the recognition of the qualified expert as a guide in momentous decisions; and in practice these decisions will have to be made on issues of public policy. Here is indeed a crucial test of a nation's political maturity. What can be imagined more difficult than the problem of combining expert judgment with popular sovranty expressed in votes? We cannot forecast the scope and course of efforts in this direction: but good statesmen and citizens will do well to keep their eyes open to the signs of the time. What little I have to say, timidly and haltingly, on the subject forms the matter of the following essay.

I F Politics is at best but a rude approximation to an Art, its operation being conditioned by what we call Human Nature, a force little understood and not easy to define, it is not to be expected or wished that the Biologists should be silent. Surely they have something to say. And what they do say has a peculiar interest from my present point of view, since their researches involve an historical process. Seeking to explain the present for the benefit of the future, they are compelled to look into the past. Inquiring into Life in all its forms, they come to the case of Man, which they treat on zoological lines. Reaching significant conclusions as to the omnipotence of heredity, historically established, they are alarmed at the public neglect of truths on which the welfare of future generations seems to them to depend. The ignorance and blindness of statesmen seems to them inexcusable, and no wonder; for they on their part regard mankind as human animals, not as voters. Now, if we recognize human nature as a dominant force in Politics, the biological view of men and their possibilities must surely be instructive. If political failures are in any degree due to human incapacity, it is madness to leave the results of biological study out of account. We must not be deterred by a foreboding of the pessimistic atmosphere awaiting us. On the other hand we may reasonably expect to find evils somewhat overdrawn in statement, as is only natural in the utterances of

---

[1] Several matters connected with the subject of this essay are dealt with in Appendices K L M, and in the separate chapter on Benjamin Kidd.

gloomy prophets whose first task is to rouse a stolid audience of the ill-informed. They have got to 'make our flesh creep', and so they do.

No topic is more vigorously handled on biological lines than the relations of social classes and their place in a political system. Their past history, their present condition in civilized states, and the probable results of the present situation in the near future, all come under review. The biologists, inspired by the scientific study of breeding in animals and plants, are convinced that the fitness or unfitness of living things to carry on their several functions is only to be explained in connexion with Heredity. Parents normally transmit their qualities to their offspring, and careful experiments in breeding indicate that transmission follows ascertainable laws. This confirms the principles on which professional breeders have long acted, and recalls to life the criticisms of ancient writers, who did not scruple to apply the experience of stock-raising to the case of Man. Accordingly the biologist turns to the human society around him, and is appalled at the spectacle. The laws of life, inexorable as he holds them to be, find no place in the state system. They are simply ignored, and he is not prepared to wink at this ignorance. Already the sincere observer can detect the evil consequences of this policy of heedless drifting. If it is allowed to continue, it is only a question of how soon civilization will totter to a final crash. In the past, classes representing superior qualities of some kind have been the leaders and rulers of men. They have guided mankind down to a time when material inventions have played havoc with old class-distinctions. The magnates of finance and trade have displaced the landowning aristocrats of the old school, but they are unable to fill the place once filled by their predecessors. There is now no link of sympathy between rich and poor. How should there be? To the poor man it seems that his labour and his necessities are exploited by the rich adventurer for his own profit. The new rich can only play a part in politics by courting the poorer masses, to whom a supreme voting power has been gradually given by repeated extensions of the franchise. The consequence is that the middle class, from which the greater part of the needful ability is produced for the service of the community, is being squeezed out between Capitalists and Proletariate. The extremes gratify their own selfish aims most easily by sacrificing to each other the interests of those who belong to neither.

The grim importance of this process is only to be fully grasped by remembering that human Society is in fact heterogeneous, and exists through its own heterogeneity. It is this heterogeneity that makes it comparable to a living organism: an analogy[1] so closely pressed that it is (I think) not without some influence on the course of the argument. In particular it is necessary that there should be a class whose function is the supply of labour as labour, without which society could not exist. In the ranks of such a class no high standard of intellect is required. And, as things are, inquiry shews that it is

[1] This analogy is further dealt with in Appendix K.

in fact[1] not found. Here we reach a dilemma, in considering modern practice. If this numerous class is to be entrusted with political power (say, supremacy,) prudence suggests that its average mental and moral standard should at least not be lowered. Otherwise, its capacity for intelligent and honourable political action will surely be impaired. If we go out of our way to create or extend means by which its more intelligent members may rise into the class above them, are we not lowering the standard of the remainder while at the same time we admit them to power? Are we not engaged in making the masses more proletarian, progressively intensifying a real political danger? The cry for equality of opportunity is urgent, no doubt. But opportunity is of use only to those who can profit by it. Now, modern practice tends to provide opportunity for all. Its lamentable result is to push forward into a presumably 'upper' class a number of young persons of second-rate or third-rate quality. They might have been a wholesome leaven in their class of origin: as it is, they only serve to lower the morale of their acquired class. Nor, I admit, need anyone deny that the conversion of the sturdy hand-worker's son into a clerk is a poor result of 'education': but the biologist means much more than this.

The challenge to the policy of modern civilized states

[1] See W McDougall, *National welfare and national decay* (1921) pp 62 foll, on some American statistics, and Lothrop Stoddard, *The revolt against Civilization* (1922) chapter ii. Whether these statistics can be taken to prove that all the men classed as of low intelligence are such by heredity, and therefore incapable of producing a superior offspring, I am not sure.

amounts to this. They are living on experiments blindly and hastily conducted, the assumption underlying which is an equality undefined and not even sincerely believed in, an equality which Science has no choice but to deny. To me the crucial question[1] at this stage seems to be, whether the modern policy, fully considered, is precisely, in principle and practice, the same as that which Science must condemn. We should not forget that a permanent specialization of classes is a notion of great antiquity and that it filled an important place in Greek political theories. It is not the same as a caste-system, though the two have points in common. It was surely less difficult to apply it in small communities (such as the states of ancient Greece) than it would be on a large scale. Yet I cannot point to a single instance of its proving a success in practice; that is, in the long run. Gild-organizations, whether voluntary or (as in the later Roman Empire) compulsory, are a quite different thing. The perpetuation of a general labour-class takes no heed of differentiation by variety of handicrafts. Granting that hands to perform simple tasks, sometimes heavy, are a necessity in any community, are modern states rashly trying dangerous experiments in their dealings with this labour-class, without seeing what they are doing? If so, to what extent? And, are there no compensating benefits to set off against the probable dangers?

[1] That there is an antagonism between democratic opinion and scientific truth, and that the former is sure to prevail, is the view of Sir H Maine *Popular Government* (ed 1909) pp 37, 190. 'Equality' is well discussed by Hearnshaw, *Democracy at the crossways,* (1918) pp 30-1.

Once we begin to criticize the view of necessary classes, a number of questions force themselves upon us and call for candid answers. Is not the division of society into three classes, upper middle and lower, imperfect— so imperfect as to be misleading? Does not the so-called lower class (that is, all below a professional standard,) include very various elements which it is unscientific to confuse? Do not its better elements produce citizens of high quality, sometimes of distinguished merit? And, what evidence is there that the men risen from their ranks do lower the morale of the governing classes? Self-sufficient and hasty they are apt to be, but I fancy historians will not allow them a monopoly of these defects in the past. Do not they *per contra* add some strength to the governing classes? Again, whence did the upper classes come? Few indeed are the old families[1] able to place at the service of the state a well-tested equipment of traditions and capacity inherited from a long roll of ancestors. The staple of our governing or upper classes now consists of men more or less 'on the make'. Selfish views of policy are their temptation, no doubt: but was not the same true of the landed aristocracy whom they have superseded? Would it be wise to aim at keeping them in power by artificial legislation, as we once did the landowners? Would an infusion of men risen from below seriously lower their mental and moral average? I dare not affirm it.

Now, in modern 'self-governing' states governing

[1] See C H Pearson, *National life and character* (1894) pp 74–8.

means leading, and it is urged that a servile deference to the turbid aspirations of the ignorant and degraded masses—demagogy, in short,—is already the cause of pernicious policy, and likely to be more so. That there have been, and will be, bad leaders, is true enough. But is not the picture somewhat overdrawn? Are the masses so very ignorant and degraded as is suggested? If so, are they obstinately content with that condition? Do they not at times shew a commonsense that redeems some of their errors? If they think that the past policy of their 'betters' has had something to do with their present defects, and resent it, perhaps with excessive impatience, is there not some excuse for them? The more we try to look straight at our present evils and the problems that arise therefrom, do we not feel more and more driven to the conclusion that the main source of our troubles[1] is the urban situation? And is not this the product of Capitalism, crude and heedless of all save immediate profit, left free to pursue selfish aims without control or check? Is it strange that the Socialist orator finds an eager audience among those who cannot live near to their work without living in sordid and unwholesome[2] surroundings, seldom or never refreshed by quiet, only relieved by occasional excitements, usually rough and often costly? Is it not a wonder that they are as peaceful as they are? Is it not a humiliating fact

[1] Cf Arnold Toynbee, *Industrial Revolution* (ed 1908) p 234.
[2] W Lawler Wilson, *The menace of Socialism* (1909) p 99, remarks that masses of manual workers live under conditions of virtual equality bordering on Communism. There is some truth in this.

that the people of our congested slums are being bred
to be fit for no other life than this, and that no other
country, not even our own Colonies, is willing to receive[1]
them as immigrants? And yet they are not of bad stock,
nor did they wilfully create this situation for themselves.
The situation is one to which I believe past history
affords no sort of parallel.

It is useless to lament the *laissez faire* blindness of
nineteenth-century politicians. They could not guess to
what horrid results the movements of their time were
tending, that growing economic prosperity was being
achieved at the cost of social and racial peril, at least
unnecessary in amount, perhaps not necessary at all. In
our slow British way we are at last awakening to our
danger; let us hope, not too late. The menace of communistic socialism was needed to supply the needful
alarm. So far, this communistic creed has not stood
criticism well. That is, it has not persuaded the majority
that the stimulus of individual property can be abolished
without general disaster. But this is a merely negative
result. There are however beginnings of a positive endeavour to improve and humanize the conditions of
industrial life. A few large capitalists have created model
villages to house in decent comfort those who work in
their factories. More recently, the Garden City movement has begun the direct employment of joint-stock

---

[1] This reluctance, and its reasons, to which I return below, is
strikingly illustrated by the lecture of Professor C K Clarke,
reported in the *Times* of 25 May 1923, and discussed in a leading
article of 26 May.

capital in providing new townships, planned from the first to promote industrial life under cheerful and healthy conditions. And, so far, these enterprises are successful; but their scale is small, compared with the evils they seek to remedy. Yet it is surely a blessed thing that a process of reaction against former indifference has been begun. It is not merely industrial; it is a moral reaction against the tacit but widespread contempt for philanthropic effort that has been the dark side of 'orthodox' Political Economy.

In all reform movements, reactions against ascertained evil influences, it is above all things necessary for the reformers to look deeply, if they mean to get a clear notion of what it is they seek to reform. Judged by this standard, it seems to me that the present attempts to improve industrial surroundings are a movement of a higher order than that for the repeal of the corn laws. No doubt Cobden was honest and patriotic, but his contribution to industrial development, immediately effective from a purely industrial point of view, offered no security for the human wellbeing of handworkers; indeed it left them more than ever exposed to the non-human working of economic laws. The lapse of time has betrayed this defect. The cause championed by Ebenezer Howard and others stands on a sounder foundation, striving to combine humanity with industrial efficiency, hoping to secure and strengthen both. It does not regard the individual man as merely a producer at whatever cost to himself; nor merely as a voter. It claims for him a possibility of decent home life,

A hopeful design 67

in which his children may grow up to be at least as good producers and good citizens as himself. It seeks to apply human intelligence and forethought for the benefit of all, and holds that acquiescence in the results of a drifting policy is not a human necessity, but an error that mankind is by its own efforts[1] able to redeem. It gives no countenance to communistic socialism, but aims at preserving under wholesome conditions the stimulus of personal acquisition. Indirectly it favours the friendly cooperation of operative hands and capitalist directors of labour, a remedy for our industrial maladies which our advisers are never tired of prescribing.

But at present this movement has not gone far, and it probably has its limits. All industries are not equally suited for such treatment. All places are not equally fit sites for Garden cities. The concentration of markets in particular places, and the local affinities of particular industries, not to mention vested interests, warn us not to expect swift transformation. But we may reasonably hope that removal of works (even on a small scale) to better surroundings, and evidence of public benefit therefrom, will tend to promote improvement in congested urban centres. If this tendency be allowed time in which to become operative (a needful reservation), it may well serve as a means of real civic betterment. And it is with the hope of arresting degradation of citizens and making it easier for them to take an intelligent part in forwarding their own welfare, and therewith the

[1] So Arnold Toynbee, *Industrial Revolution* (ed 1908) p 190, E Scott, *Men and thought in modern history* (1920) p 199.

welfare of all, that I am concerned. Mere legislative palliatives, such as 'robbing hen-roosts', may give illusive temporary relief, or stop clamour. But they leave the labourer-citizen where they found him, to be allured by the offers of shallow demagogues. And in the long run they are directly harmful, through waste of resources that might some day have been scientifically used to good purpose.

That the highest and most lasting result of schemes for improving industrial surroundings would be, not mere financial success, but to uphold and elevate the character of labourer-citizens, is my belief. I cannot cite historic instances of such an effect produced by such a cause. Modern statesmen have no doubt done much in Denmark and Switzerland to better the condition of their people by sound training and adaptation of institutions; they have their reward, but the cases are hardly analogous to ours. The methods of the German government did wonders in educating and disciplining a great nation, but it is not clear that they were favourable to the development of political capacity. The English-speaking community in which public policy is most steadily directed to insuring good conditions of life for all citizens, is New Zealand. But circumstances there make the problem so simple that comparison is idle. And some confirmation of my belief may be found in a negative consideration: it is at least sufficiently clear that a policy of letting things slide has made them worse.

I have been harping on the training of citizens deliberately, because I see no other effective means of securing a healthy political life. And schooling, of which nowadays so much is made, is only a part of training. Preparation for the work of life begins much earlier than school, and the impressions of childhood received in the home are less easily forgotten than school lessons. The importance of a decent home is beginning to be fully recognized. But the phenomenon of falling birth-rate, and its observed connexion with a higher standard of living, suggest to me a question to which some one of Galton's followers[1] might not unprofitably give his attention. It is this: is it or is it not the case that the children in large families develope their qualities on the whole better than those in small ones, though the latter may presumably receive more individual care? The connexion of this question with my main subject is remote, but the point raised is not trivial. For some biological opinion sees a prospective benefit in restriction of births, and the matter calls for further inquiry. Of course the restriction is meant chiefly if not wholly for 'undesirables' of various kinds. But I am sure that this subject needs much fuller discussion from more than one point of view. And the practical issue is this: you can do nothing without power, which implies legislative action. How can you hope to obtain the needful power, save from general consent? How can you hope to get a sufficiently general consent to action, however wise and beneficial, save from a people proud of their country, eager to promote its welfare, willing to listen to reason?

[1] The question is touched in Galton's *Inquiries into Human Faculty* ed 1907 p 213.

We need not sigh for a benevolent despot or an enlightened aristocracy. Autocrats and nobles have had
their chance, and British experience does not invite us
to revive them.

That the power required must be sought internally,
is a truism. There is no external power available for
internal reform. This truth is however liable to be
obscured by an attractive biological analogy[1], that between bodily and social organisms. The scientific breeder
finds that organisms are composed to a great extent of
separate factors or 'elements', by virtue of which they
possess their various characters or attributes. These
factors are detachable, and may be recombined in various
ways. He also notes the polymorphism of man, and holds
that what makes human society possible is this endless
variety of types and strains. These have their several
functions, and their continuation as differentiated parts
of society is necessary for its existence. But as parts or
factors of society they are treated as group-types—classes,
in short—not as individuals. Yet it is as individuals
that the breeder-specialist seems compelled to consider
them. You may detach factors from bodily organisms,
you may recombine them variously, under scientific
regulation. But 'detachment' in this sense does not imply
separation from the living body (which would mean
death). It is no more than the recognition and cultiva-
tion of selected factors, combined with elimination of
other factors, with a view to control of variation. How
this principle can be applied to the classes of a society,

[1] See the criticisms cited in Appendix K.

is far from clear. Take for instance sailors and mechanics, two classes more true to type than most. I can understand an attempt to control the variation of individuals within these classes: but how to control the variation of the classes within the general society is a very different matter. In the case of bodily organisms, the selection and control is not a function automatically developed by the unaided organism, but exercised by an external power. But in the case of human societies it is, as I have already remarked, not easy to find such a power to undertake the business in hand.

It may be said that to control the variations of individuals within their several classes, and thereby presumably to increase the class-efficiency, will ultimately result in benefit to the whole society. It will promote contentment, and so tend to general harmony. But in order to do this it will surely have to get rid of class-selfishness, a step for which I cannot find that any provision has been made. If by regulation you raise the standard of the lower class, are you not likely to make them more self-conscious and less willing to accept continued social inferiority? Persuasion to that effect will probably not be a simple matter. Let us not forget that the biological view starts by recognizing inequality of qualities in individuals of all species. Therefore it also points to a corresponding inequality in social classes, and this is I believe on the whole true. But is there not also inequality among members of the classes? Do we not assume it in contemplating their improvement through scientific regulation? And, if we reject communistic socialism as lacking the healthy stimulus of property, do we not in the same breath admit the utility of a 'natural' ambition? These questions need satisfactory answers, if our aims are to be practical and clear. Again, if we shun the unscientific error of attributing human diversity to diverse conditions of life; if we hold that 'conditions of life provide opportunity for the development of characters, but cannot increase the original endowment'; are we not still left with the task of ascertaining what that original endowment is?

Now we cannot cut the knot by simply denying that original endowment of a higher quality is ever found among the lower class. Science would never stoop to so mean a perversion of facts. It would seem that in any social system of which we have any knowledge, or any that we believe to be theoretically possible, there must be openings[1] for men to rise into a higher class or sink into a lower. If so, the best we can do is to see that the interchange takes place with the minimum of friction and hardship. We must not suffer opportunities for the development of characters to be so garbled and put out of gear by selfish interests that a man has no chance of rising. We must be careful not to favour influences that tend to precipitate his fall. By clumsy and tentative methods we do in fact attempt to discharge something of these duties; the first by our jumble of scholarship-

---

[1] W Lawler Wilson, *The menace of Socialism* (1909) p 48, says 'When the rise of intelligence to higher levels is forbidden, social stagnation ensues in the superior class, and social irritation in the inferior class'. So far I can agree with him.

system and competitive or qualifying tests, the second by progressive humanizing of the law. We are now beginning to concern ourselves with deliberate improvement of the conditions of life, virtually confessing that opportunities, to be effective from the point of view of the common good, must be something more than schools and examinations. In other words, we are alarmed at the pass to which crude capitalist exploitation has brought us, while sober men can see no way out of the social jungle by the blind alley of socialism. Yet we cannot fairly regard as criminals the generations whose policy has left us face to face with an appalling problem. To curse self-seeking is futile: we cannot abolish it, and it is only baneful when some men are allowed to destroy the opportunities of others. For Human Rights, however much stump-orators may caricature them, are after all not an idle dream in human societies. The pioneers of industrial expansion could not forecast the future virulence of the slum-plague. Even now, when we are tasting the bitter fruits of the tree of *laissez faire*, perhaps all would not agree that, evil as they are, they could have been avoided. Does the exploitation of material resources imply the exploitation of human beings? Some would answer that it is a question of degree. Now, if this be so, here is a rational ground for remedial action, a vindication of the philanthropic efforts of idealists.

In considering the passage of individuals from class to class we must not forget those who sink. If those who rise are likely to lower the morale of their new company, may not those who sink have an elevating effect on theirs? The question sounds ridiculous, but perhaps is not wholly so. We ordinarily assume that to sink is simply and solely the penalty of vice, or of some native imbecility too great for human society to condone. But I was in my youth a witness of the last scenes of a rustic tragedy, the extinction of the few remaining small landowners. Honesty and hard work could not save them. They sank into the class of local wage-earning labourers, as others in the village had done a few years earlier, or they went off to serve other men elsewhere. Now those who stayed on as labourers were the pick of the class into which they sank. Accustomed to industry and thrift, their traditions upheld them for their lifetime in dignified patience and virtue. Their fall was not their fault. Like the men of special trades in the village, they died out under the stress of economic laws. True, to sink out of a cultured class into a ruder one is perhaps more fatal to the sunken individual. Change of environment is necessarily a shock: qualities hitherto of value are henceforth in less demand: and, as those who sink are seldom young, the effect on them is apt to be disheartening, in the long run degrading. Yet it is a calumny to label all such people as mere victims of their own misconduct or weakness. That some of them do help to raise the morale of the company into which they sink, is a proposition which even the narrow range of my own observation forbids me to deny.

Another matter seems to me not undeserving of inquiry, supposing such an inquiry to be possible. I fear it is impossible: still the question it raises is significant, if biological principles are to have weight in deciding what a society should do or not do with the aim of promoting its own welfare through the welfare of its own components. The biologist, struck by the endless varieties of the human species, marvels 'that the more divergent castes of civilized humanity are capable of interbreeding and of producing fertile offspring from their crosses'. And yet they are so capable, as we all know. Many of us have known instances of the fact. Under 'feudal' conditions they were probably frequent and unconcealed. In modern times they have been sufficiently notorious to engage the attention of novelists. Illegitimate children, it is true, have less prospect of survival to maturity than the legitimate have. Still, a number of them do grow up and take their place in the class of their several mothers. Do these 'by-blows' on the whole tend to elevate or degrade the 'caste' to which social traditions have assigned them? I do not see how we are to find the answer to this question. But there it is, another witness to the complexity of the social problems awaiting the student of society. It may serve as a further warning, if more are needed, of the extreme caution with which biological principles should be applied in political practice.

No wonder then that the earnest biologist will have nothing to do with hasty legislative schemes. His honest pessimism sees no legislative organ capable of effecting a great and beneficial revolution by its own intelligence and power. The more representative Parliament becomes, the more unintelligent (as things are) it is and

will be. Therefore, when he does suggest any ameliora-
tion of existing conditions, it is rather of a negative
character; abstention from measures that are in their
working mischievous 'experiments'. Such for instance
are the present rules governing death duties, which need
remodelling on eugenic grounds, so as to favour de-
scendants whose family record promises excellence. Of
direct interference by the State, or by public opinion,
with the ordinary practices and habits of our society,
he has a profound mistrust. Even of proposals[1] to re-
strain 'defectives' from breeding, though he approves
them, he speaks with a scientific reserve. In short his
attitude is that of one who is rather shy of action, for
fear of not meeting with capable agents. As a political
utterance for present use, this conclusion leads to a bitter
condemnation of democracy.

Though the argument forces us to admit that the
existing situation is one of grave danger, is there no
alternative to acquiescence in fatalistic despair? Have
we not in the past removed grave abuses with good
results, for instance in our factory legislation? What
excuse have we for folding our hands and making inevitable that which now seems so? Reforms were hard
to carry, for want of driving-power to overcome opposition quickly: but now the driving-power is ample,
and only needs to be well directed. All (practically) now

[1] Bateson, *Biological fact* pp 13–4. From Prof Barnett's book
(see above, p 43) it seems that the proposed sterilization of
criminals has been mooted in Oregon. Barnett pp 35, 119.
Compare the remarks of Prof E W MacBride, reported in the
Times of 6 Jan 1923.

have votes, but can we say that in practice all have equal political power? Votes are given under guidance of some kind, and the question is how and by whom the guidance is to be supplied. Government being no longer a function reserved to the upper and middle classes, it is incumbent on those classes to win back by their merits as leaders the power which they no longer have as voters. If they bestir themselves, their inherited gifts will surely not degenerate through being kept in constant exercise. If they are content to slumber or idly to curse the unspeakable democracy, of course the game is up, and we drift to our doom. If the superior classes are to be submerged through their own apathy and lack of nerve, this will probably indicate an atrophy of the qualities that once made them superior. In itself their fall would perhaps not justify deep regret, but to their race and country it would be disastrous. But I hold it premature to accept such a picture as the one true view of the present situation.

There remains to consider the all-important element of time. It may be admitted that Great Britain still contains the human material for a rally to meet an impending peril, and yet it may be argued that the effort would now be made too late. Circumstances, the legacy of past neglect and blundering, may turn out to be an obstacle that no available energy can surmount. Perhaps it is fair to reply that you cannot test this without trying; but it is also fair to add that the retort does not carry us far on the path of confidence. A more daunting reflexion is what I may call the coal argument.

78   The nineteenth century 'boom'

It is asserted, and not without truth, that our present industrial phenomena are of very recent[1] origin. It so happened that England was able to turn her convenient coalfields to account at a moment when other countries were either recovering from the exhausting effects of long warfare or were as yet undeveloped and in lack of hands. Hence a temporary 'boom', on which we have traded as if it were going to last for ever. This was not merely a financial error. An unthrifty use of our resources was in fact accompanied by a heedless indifference to the means employed in their exploitation by individuals in a hurry to become rich. The consequences of this neglect took some time to make themselves felt: but now we feel them terribly. They are now so firmly established as a necessary part of our national existence that we fear to touch them, lest we starve by the way. The conclusion from this set of premises is that the doings of some two or three generations, seeking temporary profit, have set us in an evil way leading inevitably to ruin. For to halt means to lose present trade (which is our bread) and trade once lost will be lost for ever.

Is there any answer to this indictment? I can see no sincere comfort to be had in the form of challenging the several points as overstatements. The truth of the main charge will still remain. Analogies would not help our judgment much, and I know of none. It is a new story. Let me add a few considerations that shew how

[1] See the remarks of Sir H Maine, *Popular Government* (ed 1909) p 150, on the great luck of England since 1800.

serious the situation really is, in prospect of the approaching[1] development of resources similar to our own, but infinitely larger, in other countries. I omit the already active competition of American coal and labour. It is only necessary to point to the boundless coalfields and teeming populations of China and southern Russia. Those resources will not always be ineffective as they now are through political disorder. Can we, before this menace becomes actual and pressing, find time to set our house in order, enabling a later generation to face a revolution of industrial circumstances without sheer disaster and disgrace? Are we men enough for the task? Neither sufficiency of time nor our own capacity can be ascertained without trial. Evidently the first thing is to take stock of the means at our disposal for profiting by what may be only a short respite, and the next to see that we do use those means promptly and to good purpose.

That the problem must be approached from this point of view seems already to be the conviction of many philanthropic persons. Hence arise various projects based on the utilization of 'Imperial resources'. Emigration to British Colonies under skilled direction is to relieve the pressure of over-population in the mother country, to fill up vast vacant spaces within the Empire, and to bind its parts together by economic interests and the unifying ties of racial sympathy. The Barnardo Homes are a notable instance of organizations steadily working in this direction. These endeavours are however as

[1] See Appendix L.

steadily checked by the unwillingness of the great self-governing Colonies to receive just what the old country is willing to send. Both sides want only the best, and there is the ever-present risk of a deadlock. Accordingly some observers deplore[1] the policy of the last generation of British statesmen in handing over vast territories to Colonial governments with no reservation of Imperial rights. What Great Britain acquired as a great world-power, often at great cost, is now left to the free disposal of local governments, representing populations at present comparatively scanty, and generally actuated by the same narrow and selfish motives that have landed the mother country in her present plight. A notable spokesman of this school is M[r] C R Enock, who does not confine his utterances to exposing past errors, but manfully suggests[2] a remedy. His plan is that British local authorities should acquire large blocks of Colonial land, and on these should settle chosen bodies of emigrants. With these emigrants the several Home municipalities should be permanently in touch. Part of each land-block should be reserved as their common property, and serve to relieve the pressure of rates at home. A system of regulated perpetual leases on beneficial terms should guarantee the tenure of the rest, giving ample scope for individual enterprise, and yet not allowing the fortunes of any such society to be clouded by the sinister operation of land-monopoly. He is careful to add that no violation of Colonial sovranty is intended: any such community

[1] See Disraeli's remarks cited by W Sichel, *Disraeli* pp 205–6.
[2] In *An Imperial Commonwealth* (London 1910).

would be subject to the Colonial government. But the choice of emigrants would rest with the several Home municipalities that sent them out and made provision for giving them a good start. The date of these proposals in book form is 1910. Since then there has been the great war, and its momentous sequels.

The picture is an attractive one, but I think that its back-ground, if made clearer in detail, would reveal practical difficulties so great as to destroy hope of its realization. If the needful capital could be raised in the way suggested (of which in 1923 I have grave doubts), I do not think that sufficient allowance is made for the host of specialists and officials that would be required to set the business going on sound principles. For it seems contemplated that all sorts of men and women (barring downright 'undesirables'), and not merely farm-workers and domestic servants, should be included in these new settlements. And to start such communities, having a complex civilized society in each from the very beginning, would surely be an enterprise demanding unusual directive skill. Engineers, surveyors, builders, artisans in the several trades, will be needed as well as unskilled hands; and in new surroundings, if the people are to adapt themselves speedily to the climatic and other conditions, they can hardly do without scientific helpers. They cannot at once rival the knowledge of the old colonists, which has been bought by long and trying experience. Now the best specialists will only sacrifice their prospects at home on the faith of better ones abroad, and this implies that remuneration will have to be on a scale so liberal that no British municipality would feel justified in granting it. The whole scheme, admirable as an aspiration, seems to be based on a misconception of the character and position of British local governing bodies. They can hardly impose a burden on the ratepayers for the purpose of sending away some of the most efficient, and leaving the remainder chargeable with the whole cost of maintaining the infirm and unemployable poor. Yet this is how a proposal of this kind would certainly appear to the ratepayers. And all the more certainly, so long as the crushing weight of war-burdens depresses them.

Nevertheless, hopeful projectors are still (Dec 1922) advocating emigration schemes, some of them on the same general lines as Mr Enock. The new Minister of Labour calls for the cooperation of all kinds of public bodies to promote 'associational' emigration[1]. He thinks that we ought now to be able to do something better than the emigration of individuals, self-sufficient pioneers, as practised in the nineteenth century. From this he passes to suggestions that echo those of Mr Enock, and even appeals to Birmingham and Manchester, nay, even to Oxford and Cambridge, for active support. The same number of the *Times* in which his utterance is reported (20 Dec) gives also an article by an eminent Australian, pointing out the desire of the Commonwealth and its

[1] The favourable mention of the 'group-plan' at the Imperial Conference of Oct 1923 shews that schemes of this character have a great attraction for responsible statesmen. But this hardly implies approval of the municipal basis.

component States for British immigrants, and the liberal measures passed to attract them. But from his account it is quite plain that the immigrants are wanted on the land, to fill up vacant spaces and develope 'back blocks'. Artisans are not invited, and the admission that 'the Labour[1] Governments of the Dominions are not anxious to encourage immigration' as plainly tells us why. In the meantime we in England are being constantly and justly warned that agriculture here is in a dreadfully bad way, and reminded[2] that we cannot do without it. Temptation will appeal to the more vigorous of our farmers and farm-workers: how shall we fare, if left with only the weaker and less enterprising? And is the first outlay likely to be the whole burden of public bodies that undertake to establish 'associational' settlements? The old-style pioneer took his chances. In case of failure, he knew that he had nothing to fall back upon at home, and must find another job in the new country or sink into a wastrel. In keeping the settlers in touch with the public body at home, are we not likely to weaken the self-reliance of disappointed men? Such cases[3] will surely occur, and with them complaints that the prospects of success have been delusively overdrawn.

[1] Compare a message from Western Australia in the *Times* of 27 July 1923, and another of 11 Oct, giving the Australian Manufacturers' contrary view, calling for artisans.

[2] Especially interesting to me is *Our English land muddle, an Australian view*, by Frank Fox, published in 1913 or 1914.

[3] In the *Times* of 24 July 1923 is a significant message from Melbourne reporting the attempts of immigrants to return to England as stowaways. An earlier case *ibid* 27 Dec 1922, commented on 28 Dec.

Noble and well-meant as the Minister's suggestions are, I doubt whether he, any more than Mr Enock, is well-advised in relying on public bodies to carry out a plan of this kind. Manchester and Birmingham may see their way to finding the capital and the men and women for the purpose. Oxford and Cambridge are only kept going on their present scale by public grants out of the taxes. As public bodies, what can they do? If it is proposed to use tax-money for 'associational' settlements, they will be among the tax-payers, and will need a further grant to enable them to pay their share of the cost of exporting their fellow-citizens. Meanwhile Manchester and Birmingham will perhaps desire free entry of their manufactures into Australia, if they are to find capital for a venture that, if successful, would enlarge the Australian home-market to the advantage of Australian home-manufactures. I feel bound to set forth difficulties of this kind, because they are real. But I am not hinting that they are fatal. It is the risk of attempting too much at once, with means of doubtful efficiency, that seems to me serious. A gigantic scheme, pushed forward by platform propaganda, is very likely to be undertaken in too hopeful a spirit, without full recognition of obstacles to be encountered. And a gigantic failure would leave things much worse than it found them. Small beginnings, tentative and subject to the hard test of time, would either encourage larger enterprises or deter public bodies from using public funds injudiciously. Subscriptions of a philanthropic or half-philanthropic character will not be less available because

Need of good will and good leading 85

the risk of loss is accompanied by the possibility of a dividend. The Garden City movement shews this. And the after-effects of the great war should teach us that cautious policy, not frantic effort, is the need of the hour.

The two fundamental problems, for which only a moral solution can serve, are these. In the Colonies, the Imperial government (whatever that expression may mean) has given up all claim to control the assignation of land. Therefore it cannot grant rights to its own emigrants. It rests solely with the Colonial governments to fix the conditions on which they will admit new settlers. Here is an opening for the exercise of good will rather than hard bargaining. In the mother country, suffering has bred discontent to such a degree that communistic agitators get a hearing, and many thousands are more eager to redistribute old wealth (and to destroy much of it in the process) than to create new. Nothing can check this tendency but the spread of a firm conviction that it leads to common ruin. There is happily so far no reason to believe that the masses have gone mad and are deaf to commonsense considerations. If the British 'intellectuals' have the courage to assert themselves, there is no ground for despair. The main thing is to gain time for things to rearrange themselves gradually and peaceably. That there will be changes in industry and in society generally, I take to be beyond a doubt: but this is a condition to which human societies have had to adapt themselves, slowly or swiftly, from time immemorial. If Great Britain and her offshoots cannot learn to work together by mutual accommoda-

tion, then, I admit, the 'British Empire' is likely to
fail, and in it the grandest experiment ever made for
the instruction of the human race. But the end is not yet.

No—Science has not said her last word. She must
bear her part boldly, not standing aloof in sublime disgust. As Economics, she must convince the handworkers
that they, as much as the headworkers, are bound by
irresistible natural laws. As Biology, she must expose the
fallacies that hide the truths of heredity, and remind
mankind that mere animalism has made the other
animals the slaves and victims of Man. Neither Historians
nor Statesmen, nor their readers and constituents, can
dispense with the positive and disinterested aid of scientific
inquiries. That is, if Science is meant for Man, rather
than Man for Science.

But, when all is said and done, we are driven back
to the admission that our hopes must rest upon a moral
change, far-reaching enough to affect the thoughts and
the conduct of all classes of society. It was once the
fashion to hold that to present the need of amendment,
and the prospect of benefit from reform, soberly and
logically, was enough. If not the only thing to be done,
it was so much the most important thing that all else
was of little avail. Men would surely listen to reason
and act by the guidance of reason: if they did not, there
was an end of the matter. But Psychology, creeping into
History, is more and more disclosing the vital truth that
reforms in the past, often praised as triumphs of reason
and justice, have in fact been achieved by the forces
of interest and passion. It is becoming clear that, if

practical results are to be attained, it is to the emotional side of human nature that leaders of men must appeal. Unhappily the record of recent generations does not encourage us to hope that a supply of statesmen psychologically gifted will at once be found equal to the demand. Misunderstanding of the influences really effective in other peoples has long been epidemic among national leaders. Germany was not the only sinner in this regard. And that ministers misjudge the feeling of their own people is an ever-recurring experience. In short, from politicians as such, apart from emotional outside pressure, we must not expect much, or that soon.

This consideration naturally reminds us that a great and highly organized influence exists in the form of the religious bodies. There have of late been various movements towards a religious revival, connected with schemes for a reunion of dissident confessions. Good men believe[1] that by setting non-essentials aside, and combining on a basis of agreed essentials, a cooperative unity might be reached. The greater force and vigour thus attained would enable the joint organization to work more effectually upon the morals of a too materialistic world. Hence are drawn hopes of a general Renaissance (the word is actually used), in which humanity will redeem itself by purging its civilization of the vices and errors that imperil it today. The aspiration is noble, and the crusade against selfishness and indifference assails

[1] *The coming Renaissance*, edited and arranged by Sir James Marchant, with an introduction by Dean Inge (1923). The following paragraphs are written in consideration of these essays.

our modern evils at a very vulnerable point. But the attack will have to be made by way of emotion, and it remains to be asked how far a compromise on matters of dogma and practice is to be relied on as a step towards the enhancement of emotional force and value. It may be replied that the new movement is primarily an appeal to reason, for to discard non-essentials is a rational process. But an appeal to reason is an appeal to individual minds. How far is the liberty of thought to go? The bankruptcy of rationalism in the English Church of the eighteenth century, solemnly deriding what was called Enthusiasm, is not a reassuring spectacle.

It would seem that twentieth-century Christianity, acutely conscious of present evils and of its own duty to lead mankind in better ways, seeks strength in re-union, that it may hopefully face the task. But its first need is to make clear to all by what method the desired combination of forces is to be achieved. To reunite the several ministries will not by itself carry the movement very far. The really important point is how to make an impression on the laity, of whose indifference to religious influences these earnest reformers complain. If theological experts can agree to throw over a mass of old dogmas and symbols, and their several followers are willing to condone the jettison, will this induce the ordinary lay citizen to rally to the new-model Church? I mean, will he serve it heart and soul, and be prepared for self-sacrifice in a holy cause? If the Church officially discards some of the tenets which he personally has discarded long ago, will this suffice to arouse his enthusiasm? Will it draw him further than a tepid acquiescence? It is to be feared that a Church based on compromise of negative character may not find it easy to apply the goad of conscience to minds led by experience to expect further accommodations. The possible effect on the active members of various sects is also not to be ignored. Trained in the belief that their several creeds and usages are the best guarantee of eternal happiness for themselves, will they not be disconcerted by so serious a change of front? Will reason, justifying the change, avail to maintain their moral warmth? I confess I doubt it. The loss on this side appears to me certain, the gain in attracting the indifferent very doubtful.

Therefore when we are told[1] that 'the religion mankind needs is not a matter of knowledge but of life'; when a divine who distrusts 'ultimate and final expressions of faith' declares that 'creedal religion can never again occupy the position it has held in the past'; when a great scholar is quoted as saying 'All Christian doctrine is summed up in Christ's person, all Christian morality in Christ's example'; when a sympathetic man of science adds that 'The passive acceptance of unverified dogma is not faith at all, but credulity', while he 'cannot see that there can be faith without action'; when an eminent Doctor of Divinity, in case of his re-incarnation, 'would be a chemist and a biologist', and tells us that 'ethical philosophers and speculative divines irritate

---

[1] These quotations are from the book of essays referred to above.

but do not satisfy my reason';—surely one who wishes well to all these earnest speakers, and to the rest of his fellow countrymen also, may rub his eyes and ask 'where are we?' If all these assertions are sound in fact and reason, what next? If religious differences are to be made up in word and deed so as to satisfy these reformers, and at the same time so thoroughly and finally as to unite all the sects in arms against the evils of this present world, is it not above all things necessary to offer a simple and definite programme of union?

But in the collection of essays[1] to which I refer I find nothing precise, nothing clear, but the many negatives. For instance, I gather that the traditional doctrine of the Holy Trinity is out of date. Christ is spoken of as the 'Man of Galilee' with love and honour, but not I think frankly deified. Of the Holy Ghost I detect no mention. So I wonder whether these writers are Unitarians at heart. And looking from my own point of view, that is, the quest of moral influences likely to effect in practice some improvement in the condition of mankind, I cannot see in the movement towards reunion on these lines any assurance that the needs of the age will be met. For the first need is the supply and application of energy, driving-power, for the benefit of human society, and I hold it vain to seek this in the cool atmosphere of sober reasoning. Reformers must start from human nature as it is, and the most

---

[1] *Heralds of Revolt*, by Canon W Barry DD (new ed 1909) seems to me a book of the same negative character, non-constructive.

logical reunionist has psychologically much to learn from
the methods of the Salvation Army. If mankind are not
to slip back under the control of a dominant priesthood,
the problem is how to exert moral influence on individuals
in masses. This calls for warmth, and warmth is hardly
to be generated by the discreet repair of formulae. That
is, if religions are made for man, and not man for
religions. Still, the resources of human nature are not
yet exhausted, and it is too early to assume that future
efforts of the Churches must inevitably fail.

The power of religious conviction on masses of men
has often been illustrated by reference to the triumphant
progress of Islam in the past and its present vitality.
True, as a system it can hardly be credited with political
success in the long run, but it does not seem to be
seriously shaken by misfortune, and it still makes con-
verts. Its fatalistic bent is however too strong to qualify
it for social action as an engine of reform. More notable
still is the operation of old ancestral religion in China,
cited by a recent inquirer[1] as an example of the permanent
effect of 'religious motive'. Patriarchal, and devoted to
continuation of the Family on the strict agnatic principle
of succession in the male line, it calls for complete self-
sacrifice to attain its end. For the great bulk of a vast
population (on whom the later religious or philosophic

[1] A J Hubbard MD, *The fate of empires* (1913). He quotes
freely from an article by Prof E A Ross, University of Wis-
consin, on *The struggle for existence in China*, Century Magazine
for July 1911, a very interesting paper. See also E A Ross,
The changing Chinese (1911), and *Social Psychology* (1909),
significant books. Also below, Appendix L.

movements have had little or no influence) this accepted position means the necessity of submitting to excessive toil on miserable or hopeless terms. Under such conditions, it appears to sympathetic observers that with the increase of population an awful crisis is drawing near: at all events they remark that even slight agricultural failures produce famines and ghastly sufferings, far beyond the power of our Western imagination to conceive. Yet the ancestral system stands. It is not likely that development of resources by foreign enterprise will materially alter or annul it within any future that can reasonably be forecast. It is a part of the people's being. Exploitation may well lead to its further expansion, through increase of means; if it did, so much the larger would be the volume of yellow men seeking outlets everywhere. The picture may be overdrawn, and the fact of the writer's using it to point a contrast with the decay of the Roman agnatic family system, undermining the healthy society of early Rome, may assure us that it is at least not an understatement.

Nevertheless, it would be foolish to minimize the moral of the author's argument or disdain its lesson. That he is right in holding what he calls Religious Motive to be an effective means for promoting 'racial duty', I cannot deny. When he speaks of it as 'suprarational', and denies that a permanent civilization can be founded[1] on Reason, I am not quite convinced, but I cannot refute him. When he appraises the value of motives by the test of conduct, most honest men will

[1] See the following chapter on Benjamin Kidd.

agree with him. But from my point of view there appears a question that must not be shirked. Can his opinions on 'racial duty' be reconciled with those of the Biologists? To them improvement of the human breed is an object of desire, and to that end they would allow some control of human reproduction, exercised presumably under the guidance of Reason, and tending to put quality before quantity. To him the actual preservation of the race is the one thing essential, and other considerations would apparently have to wait until the main object is secured. In other words, the existence of a race must come first: if it is doomed to die out, attempts to maintain or improve its quality are hardly worth the making. Now the continuance of a race, for which under primitive conditions Instinct sufficiently provided, is menaced by self-regarding considerations which originate in the workings of individual Reason. 'Religious Motive' is the only influence that has as yet shewn the power of counteracting the misuse of Reason and producing some of the valuable effects of Instinct. On the practical recognition of this the permanence of civilization depends.

This argument, of which I can only give here a very inadequate outline, is not to be lightly dismissed. But it is itself an appeal to Reason, and Reason will certainly not be silenced. Mankind, however blindly, seek what they deem happiness. If wrong reasoning has led them astray, only a better reasoning can lead them right. Without a convinced belief in the truth of its fundamental principles, Religious Motive will be of no avail.

Somehow a harmony[1] must be found between the reasoning of Science and the supra-rational efficiency of what I may call for shortness Faith. How this can be attained, is beyond me to say: I only know that good ends need effective means, and that effective means, not employed for good ends, may do positive evil.

My general conclusions are therefore as follows

1. The criticisms of Biologists and social students on the condition and prospects of civilized Western peoples are in the main just, though perhaps somewhat over-drawn.

2. There is no sufficient reason for believing that the evils indicated could not be overcome by deliberate and sustained effort; but the chances of effecting this become less and less by delay.

3. In popular governments there is latent driving-power able to carry through necessary changes; the difficulty ahead is how to make this power active and keep it in action.

4. A purely rational influence will not meet the difficulty in dealing with average citizens: at the best it is too slow in its operation.

5. Therefore emotional influences are on no account to be dispensed with.

---

[1] In the *Autobiography* of Benjamin Franklin, ed 1909 by J Bigelow pp 186–206, is a very interesting account of his efforts in this direction. Rationalistic and primarily aiming at self-perfection, he eventually thought of founding a sect on a definite basis of a creed. But pressure of his public duties prevented him from putting it in practice.

6. The chief emotional influences available may be classed as religious, using the word in a large sense.

7. Religious bodies are not blind to the needs of the time: but they are rationalizing, and that timidly, however bold some of their leaders' utterances may appear.

8. If timely help is to come from their hearty co-operation for the public good, they must agree to differ on points of technical theology, and find some common footing for joint action of a more emotional philanthropic character.

9. For opportunities are slipping away while a policy of give-and-take is slowly working in the region of dogma, and there is now no unbaptized Constantine to impose provisional orthodoxy by the hand of imperial power.

BENJAMIN KIDD[1].

I HAVE been warned by a very competent adviser that I ought to refer directly to the influence of the works of Benjamin Kidd. That the views of this independent writer have not been without effect on some of those authors to whom I have referred in the essays or appendices, is very clear to me. But Mr Kidd built up nothing less than a new philosophic system, regarding the history and prospects of humanity from a point of view peculiarly his own. And it is no part of my undertaking to offer a particular criticism of his system. I do however feel bound to say something of it here. For it is a striking fact that materials of which he and the other writers make common use lead him and them to very different conclusions. His views are much the wider in their range; and, right or wrong, are evidently the fruit of contemplation not inspired by the shock of sudden alarm.

What differentiates Mr Kidd's line of argument from that of the others is his application of evolutionary doctrine. We are all evolutionists of a sort nowadays, but we differ widely in the use we make of evolutionary principles. Now most of those who apply them to the case of mankind have in view the Individual, and are concerned with racial questions of breeding as affecting the past history and future prospects of the human race. And, the more surely they are convinced of the irresistible power of heredity for good and for evil, the greater is

[1] *Social Evolution* (ed 1898), *The Science of Power* (1918), *Principles of Western Civilization* (1902).

their despair when they note the difficulty or rather the impossibility of taking practical steps to insure that the new knowledge shall be turned to account for human betterment. By enlightened and consistent effort for a few generations much might be achieved; but how is a start to be made? To bring about a momentous change in the spirit and working of a civilization, the result of untold ages, is a colossal undertaking. It will call for the exercise of overwhelming power. If we cannot discover a sufficient driving power available for the purpose, to us the future is one of blank darkness, and philanthropic inquiry ends in pessimism. Such is the position of those reformers who look to existing institutions for a means of reaching an urgently needed improvement, and who mournfully pronounce them inadequate.

Mr Kidd would solve the problem by applying the doctrine of evolution not to the Individual but to Society. Man is a social animal. As his past has been ruled for good or evil by his social necessities, so too will his future be. Taking this as a natural law, and granting that to work in harmony with nature is less wasteful and more effective than to strive against her, the true interest of mankind is clear. Viewing the present as the outcome of the past, and observing how Man's progress has often been hindered by shortsighted disregard of the future, he must learn (and in fact is gradually learning) to have an eye to the future as well as to the past. Implied in this (though I have not noted a direct statement) is the principle that Society on a healthy foundation is able to carry out by its own vigour and capacity any reforms to promote its wellbeing. If I am right in this inference, it follows that all reforms of an eugenic character, dealing with individuals and their improvement, are to be looked for as automatically assured through the operation of the Society. That is, our aim should be, not to attempt eugenic betterment by the inadequate means now available, but to increase our 'social efficiency'. It is this social efficiency that marks a superior race. With this quality in function, a future of prosperity is no idle dream.

But what is the secret of social efficiency? The answer can only be found by a sound interpretation of history. Once we discover the causes that have produced social vigour, and therewith national strength, we can see our way. It is not the dominance of Reason; for reason, left to itself, pursues a self-regarding course in the interest of the Individual. It looks only to the present, and does not contribute to the cohesion or stability of a social union. Now it is only as part of a social union of some kind that Man exists as Man, and not as a merely selfish brute. Civilized life in the past has only been possible through the workings of another influence interfering with the dominance of Reason. This is emotional. Altruism, Humanitarianism, Philanthropy, are names now in use to describe it: in any case it is ultra-rational. Above all, it is not self-regarding, and contributes directly to the cohesion and stability of social unions. This it is that creates social efficiency, and has been the means of raising the human species from a brutal level. Even now it has little open recognition. In the past it has for the most part been ignored.

Emancipation

But it was nevertheless in function, however feebly and obscurely; some consciousness of common humanity slowly grew out of the necessities of association. Needless to say, it could not flourish in ages when slavery was normal. But its unrecognized presence made civilizations stand for a time; its weakness and insufficiency led to their decay and fall.

These conclusions are supported by a version of past history, original and in some respects not easily challenged. Into details I cannot enter here. Suffice it that Mr Kidd traces a great change, suggestive of hope for the future, back to the revival of learning and especially to the Reformation of the sixteenth century. The general effect of these movements has been emancipation, the growth of a sense of personal responsibility, the setting free of social influences of an altruistic character, so that they can and do act, and are more and more in function as time goes by. Humanitarian principles and practice, in spite of temporary set-backs, do spread: and it is important to note that the peoples most effectively influenced thereby are those which have been most successful. In other words, their social efficiency has been so increased, their cohesion and stability assured, that no internal or external strain has been able to destroy their prosperity and honour. This superior quality (of Societies, not of Individuals,) is strikingly illustrated by the experience of peoples who have governed other peoples. It is on the whole those who have been most humane in their dealings that have succeeded best in a difficult task. Let me welcome this comforting assurance that the development of a public conscience is both a sweet and a profitable thing.

Now the influences that determine the onward movement of a people are in the main not rational but emotional. Such policies as our Factory Legislation or the Abolition of Slavery are more the outcome of aroused feeling than of logical debate. It is what Mr Kidd calls the 'emotion of the ideal' that bears us along. It is in its essence moral, religious in the widest sense, closely connected with the ultra-rational altruistic force of religion, particularly of Christianity, above all of Christianity freed from medieval fetters. This influence propagates itself by social heredity, a psychic development of social culture. It is not inborn and transmitted by individual inheritance, but conveyed from generation to generation by education of the young. Now this course of social development is not, like development of individuals, difficult and slow. That social change may be easy and thorough, whether for good or for evil, is shewn in the recent transformations of Japan and Germany. Let us once become practically conscious (as we are becoming) of possessing in the control and direction (not the suppression) of Emotion the means of shaping our destinies, and we may face the future with confidence. Such in effect is Mr Kidd's antidote to pessimism.

In short, all depends on a true interpretation of the law of Evolution in its application to mankind. Man is man in respect of his essentially social nature, and it is as a being existing in societies that we must regard him.

Society, healthy or unhealthy, is the condition of his weal or woe. His rise, rightly viewed, has not been effected by a selfish conflict of individual aims looking only to present interest. Such a struggle had its proper place in past ages, and served to bring the stronger races to the front. The real cause of progress has been the silent operation of an instinct unconsciously looking to the future and the common interest of the society. Such, in ages of conflict, was the breeding-instinct that assured the safety of communities by increase of numbers. But we now live in times when the military organization of society has proved a failure, when the emancipation of the excluded masses is nearly complete, privilege is disappearing, and it is becoming normal for all men to share in the rivalry of existence on equal terms. This change has been effected, not by the claimant force of the excluded (they were not strong enough for that) but through altruistic influences acting as a solvent on the grim tenacity of the classes in power. A large part of the British nineteenth-century legislation is only to be accounted for on this hypothesis. This section of Mr Kidd's argument seems to me peculiarly strong when viewed in the light of historic facts, and his estimate of the importance of Emotion as compared with Reason, as a social and political force, is borne out by the daily phenomena of public life.

Yet, while recognizing the value of the writer's sincere and independent work, I cannot accept his conclusions without some reserve. One may admit that to cooperate with nature in the evolutionary progress of

Society is wise, and that the influence of social means on the social animal is one of high potency. But I cannot escape from a conviction that the process contemplated—the conscious formation of sound social character on a basis of ultra-rational emotion, and its transmission by education,—must depend for its success on the qualities of its first promoters in a very high degree. Good movements are after all most effective in the hands of good men. Therefore the warnings of eugenic theorists as to the danger of race-degeneration in civilized societies, and their suggestions of reform, are not to be thrust into the background as secondary aims, lacking seriousness and urgency. That evolution may be used to improve individuals, no one nowadays denies. It seems to me that social means of improving Man, and human effort in improving Society, are reciprocating parts of the same great fact. You cannot correlate them as mental concepts in a logical order. We only know that Man, as animal, comes first in order of time: it is not quite a case of the chicken and the egg.

The above paragraphs deal only with those main conclusions of Mr Kidd that have a direct bearing on my subject. I am not indifferent to the happy forecasts (his first book is dated 1894) that strike the reader here and there, to his criticism of the Biologists, or to his insistence on the supreme importance of Woman in relation to the social process contemplated in his system. But to treat of such matters would not only carry me too far; I mistrust my own power of handling them to any good purpose.

In connexion with the project of conscious effort the following extract from Galton's *Inquiries into human faculty* (ed 1907 pp 197–8, first ed 1883) is of some interest. He is speaking of man's achievements on the earth, and continues thus.

'Now that this new animal, man, finds himself somehow in existence, endowed with a little power and intelligence, he ought, I submit, to awake to a fuller knowledge of his relatively great position, and begin to assume a deliberate part in furthering the great work of evolution. He may infer the course it is bound to pursue, from his observation of that which it has already followed, and he might devote his modicum of power, intelligence, and kindly feeling to render its future progress less slow and painful. Man has already furthered evolution very considerably, half unconsciously, and for his own personal advantages, but he has not yet risen to the conviction that it is his religious duty to do so deliberately and systematically'. (The closing words on p 220 reassert this view.)

I feel justified in holding that there is room for the schemes of the Social-evolutionist and the Individual-evolutionist to work side by side toward a common end.

APPENDICES

A. *Influence of personalities.*

PERHAPS I have said enough in the text on this topic. The fashion of ignoring personal agents seems to have passed away. But one point of view is not always fully recognized; I mean the attraction that past personalities have for present statesmen. It is natural that this should be so, for the man who has to act is not likely to forget that the political machine, like other machines, needs to be set going and kept going by human agency; all the more because it is a complex of human parts. To give a list of individuals whose characters and careers have undoubtedly had a marked effect on the course of history is easy. I need only refer in particular to the remarks of Bishop Stubbs (*Lectures*, pp 244–6) on Henry VIII, and add the names of Cromwell and Monk in the seventeenth century, and Walpole and the elder Pitt in the eighteenth. Foreign countries supply endless instances, perhaps none more striking than the great Italian trio, Mazzini, Garibaldi, Cavour. It may be not amiss to set down a few references to opinions of authorities who have dealt with this topic either as students of the past or as contemporary observers in recent times.

Lord Acton, *Lectures*, pp 3, 4; *Essays*, pp 320–1.
Edwyn Bevan, *Indian nationalism* (1913) pp 13, 14.
Burke, *Reflections on the Revolution in France* (ed Payne) pp 185–6.
J B Bury, *Darwinism and History*, pp 16, 17.
Lord Cromer, *Essays*, I p 93; II 79, 187; III 93.

Moral judgment 105

Archibald Forbes, *Souvenirs of some Continents* (1885), chapter on Macgahan.

S R Gardiner, *Hist Eng* 1603–42 (ed 1884) vi 340, *Preface to* vol x p x.

F Harrison, *The meaning of history* (1894) p 11.

F Inderwick, QC, *Side-lights on the Stuarts* (1888) pp 22–3.

B Disraeli, quoted by W Sichel, *Disraeli* (1904) pp 11, 19.

J S Mill, *Logic*, vi 11 §§ 1–4.

Lord Morley, *Notes on politics and history* (1913) pp 25, 37, 58, 92.

E Renan, *Vie de Jésus* (ed 1873), introduction, pp xcix-c.

J H Rose, *Nationality as a factor in modern history* (1916) p 120.

J R Seeley, *Introduction to Political Science* (1896) pp 340, 381.

Sir William Temple, *Observations upon the United Provinces of the Netherlands* (ed 1705) pp 124–5.

Graham Wallas, *The Great Society* (1914 before the War) p 307, and generally, *Human nature in Politics* (1908).

Sir Thomas Barclay, *Thirty years Anglo-French reminiscences* (1914). This interesting book has acquired a new interest since the great War. That a Scotsman, educated in both France and Germany, could do so much to promote good relations between England and France, and yet be so blind as to the real aims and intentions of the German government, is a notable phenomenon. On p 147 he gives a most illuminating description of the tangled issues of international politics and the importance of personal qualities in dealing with them.

B. *Difficulties attending moral judgment in History.*

Starting from the assumption that action taken from bad motives may produce good results—and *vice versa*—we may note a double danger:

(*a*) Too close a devotion to moral judgment may impair the strictly historical sense,

(*b*) Too 'scientific' a procedure may exclude morality altogether.

Now to steer clear of both these dangers is a task that calls for infinite discretion and self-control.

It is an obvious question, cannot historians rule morality out of court? What have moral considerations to do with the business of ascertaining effects and causes?

In reply we may point out that the need of appealing to the moral sentiments of nations is a fact, a fact which statesmen are at times compelled to recognize. In internal politics we know it well, and it finds voice in Law.

International Law is an attempt to secure wider recognition of ethical principles in world-politics, and to stabilize them in the form of an agreed system. It aims at the eventual settlement of all differences by methods juridical, not military.

It is an attempt to apply to States the rules that experience has justified in the case of individuals. What hinders it is the difficulty of finding a Sanction. Who is to be umpire between States, with power to enforce decisions?

It seems then that civilized mankind are assuming an analogy between the relations of Man to Man and those of State to State, and wishing to make a theoretical analogy real, in fact a part of normal practice.

Now in the relations of Man to Man experience of ages has established certain principles as necessary foundations of common life in societies. Without these, Law could not exist. We call them Morality. The State enforces them by penalties. True, penalties are now and then evaded, but seldom, and generally owing to the 'benefit of the doubt' when evidence is incomplete. But penalties could not be inflicted without a prevalent moral force to approve them; nor could the benefit of the doubt be granted, were it not that the possible punishment of the guiltless is too great an outrage on our human feelings. Sanctions and sentiments combine to uphold the highest standard of practical justice that a given society at a given stage of its development is capable of reaching. Perfection is not attainable. But a legal scale of penalties raises Sanctions above the irrational fluctuation of passing whims, while sentiment at need is able to mitigate the possibly revolting consequences of rigid pedantry.

Therefore, if we are to treat the assumed analogy as real, and to act on it in arranging the relations between States, we cannot avoid recognition of Right and Wrong, and shaping our course accordingly. And, if our views of Right and Wrong are the fruit of experience as regards the relations of individuals, it seems reasonable in those of States to seek some guidance from the relations between States in the past. This can only be got from impartial history; and this history must do its best to supply. History then is bound to pass moral judgments, with full allowance for time and circumstance, as a court that hears both sides and gives its decisions with dignity and reserve.

The above carries with it the further conclusion, that a purely indifferent 'scientific' attitude towards the past implies a purely fatalistic attitude towards the present, and therefore towards the future. But in our individual lives we do not adopt this attitude, nor could the world go on if we did. We learn from past successes and failures, and it is hard to see why States should not do the same. Indeed they do sometimes profit by the lessons of experience, and the record of such instances is an encouragement of value.

Here we are face to face with the old problem of Free Will, of which we need only remark that to ignore Free Will cannot serve either to interpret the past or to benefit the future. To ignore it is itself not easily distinguishable from a free-will act. And the mystery behind it is beyond our solution; to ignore it demands a proof that we cannot give.

In practice, the ethical question is apt to be obscured by economic questions. For instance, if we regard States as stable units, disregarding the phenomena of their growth and decay, we may see in Free Trade a gospel of peace. But such a stable condition has never really existed, nor does the modern system of independent States so far give sure warrant for expecting it soon. Each has its own interests, and shapes its policy from its own point of view. The Manchester school relied on the effect of international commerce as a cause of peace. But trade craves open markets, and each State wants to secure markets for its own products. Negotiation between States yields too little to satisfy keen bargainers. Hence jealousy and greed seek their satisfaction in annexation of territories, and reserving such new markets for their own citizens. This policy further emphasizes the opposition of material interest that sets States against each other: and in the long run this may tend to be a cause of war.

So long as independent States remain (and we must not ignore the good that comes of their friendly rivalry) the aim of true humanity will be to bring them, so far as possible, under the same rules as are found to be beneficial in regulating the conduct of men. If wrongs are to be prevented and peace to be maintained by a League of Nations, it must be founded on a firm moral basis. If peace promotes trade, and trade peace, economic interests and ethical force may reach a millennium of mutual support. But, disguise it as we will, the sanction of material force cannot be dispensed with in the world as we know it, whether it be States or individuals with whom a regulative power is called upon to deal. If I have stated this issue fairly, it follows that the statesman has before him a grave problem—how to apply contemporary ethics effectually so as to moderate the contemporary appetite of seekers after immediate gain. The details of the problem are ever shifting. Science finds out new sources of profit, arising from extended use of particular products. In the course of national rivalries, a new situation may be (and has been) so manipulated by one State as to give its own people a practical monopoly of a particular manufacture, calculated to insure for them an advantage in the event of war. Hence other States, conscious of impending danger, are faced by the question of 'key-industries'.

Ought they to protect such industries by tariffs? To a Free-trade country this is a serious matter, since protection of one industry is felt to be a burden on others, and in itself undesirable as presumably unfair. Under conditions of a secure world-peace the question would not (or at least need not) arise. But what present prospect is there of this? Thus the statesman, looking at the alternatives, world-peace plus Free-trade, and cautionary Protection plus security, has to choose in which direction his policy should lean. And he has to act: at some given point of time he has to find a policy effective and feasible. Unless he is content to follow simple traditions, either of 'Cobdenite' principle or of 'national' self-regard, he has no easy task; and economic considerations will be complicated by others, the balancings of expediency, in which morality plays an important part.

The following references may be of interest as specimens of the opinions of some highly qualified judges.

Lord Acton, *Lectures on Modern History*, pp 24–8, 202. *Essays on Modern History* pp 362, 436, 490–1, 500.
B Croce, *Theory and history of historiography* (Eng trans 1921) pp 86–7.
Lord Cromer, *Essays* II pp 187, 232, 330.
W A Dunning, *History of political theories Ancient and Mediaeval* (1902) discussing Macchiavelli pp 291–6. Compare Sir F Pollock, *History of the science of politics* (1911) p 43.
Lord Morley, *Notes on politics and history* (1913) p 30.
J S Mill, *Logic* VI 11 § 2.
J A R Marriott, *The European Commonwealth* (1918) p 91.
Lord Bryce, *Studies* (1901) II pp 185–6.

Nationality

S R Gardiner, *History of England* 1603–42 (ed 1883) II
p 195, *The Great Civil War* I p 9, III p 120.
J E T Rogers, *Economic interpretation of history* (1888)
pp 366, 384.
Adam Sedgwick, *Discourse on the studies of the University*
(ed II, 1834) pp 86, 89.
H Sidgwick, *Development of European polity* (1903) pp 4, 5.
Bishop Stubbs, *Lectures* (1886) p 21.
A J Toynbee, *The New Europe* (1915) pp 33, 38.
Bishop R Watson, *Anecdotes* (ed 1818) II p 194.
Lord George Hamilton, *Parliamentary reminiscences* (1917)
p 327.
B Disraeli, quoted in W Sichel, *Disraeli* (1904) p 65.
J Oakesmith, *Race and Nationality* (1919) p 255.
H G Wells, *First and last things* (ed 1917) pp 57–8.
Graham Wallas, *Our Social heritage* (1921) pp 200–4.
In the *Observer* of 19 Aug 1923 is an article *Hard-hitting
History* very much to the point on this question.

C. *Nationality and national idealism.*

This topic, as bearing on the formation and existence
of states, may be considered as outside the limits of my
proper subject. But I have had to touch upon it in the
text, and I cannot resist the temptation to refer to a
few passages in the works of writers who can speak
with authority from their several points of view.

Lord Bryce, *Race sentiment as a factor in History* (1915)
passim, but especially pp 29–32, also *Studies* I 268.
Lord Cromer, *Essays* III pp 205, 207.
B Disraeli, quoted in W Sichel, *Disraeli* (1904) pp 19, 66.
W A Dunning, *the British Empire and the United States*
(1914) p 273.
S R Gardiner, *The Great Civil War* I 224, *Cromwell's place
in history*, lecture III.

J A R Marriott, *The European Commonwealth* (1918) p 314.

Lord Morley, *Notes on politics and history* (1913) pp 40, 77.

J H Rose, *Nationality as a factor in modern history* (1916) p 120 and *passim*.

H Sidgwick, *Development of European polity* (1903) p 26.

A J Toynbee in *The Balkans* (1915) p 237 foll, *The New Europe* (1915) pp 20, 33, 38.

T F Tout, *France and England* etc (1922) p 28–9.

G M Trevelyan, *Garibaldi's defence of Rome* (1907) p 191.

J Oakesmith, *Race and Nationality* (1919, but written earlier).

Sir Henry Maine, *Popular Government* (1909) pp 27–8.

E Jenks, *The State and the Nation* (1919) p 280.

H W C Davis, *The political thought of H von Treitschke* (1914) pp 185–9.

Gustave Le Bon, *The World in revolt* (Eng trans 1921) Book VI, chapter 3, pp 197–203.

D. *Institutions, fits and misfits.*

On this simple topic it may suffice to give a few references

Lord Bryce, *Studies* I p 379.

Burke, *Reflections on the Revolution in France* (need of experience) ed Payne p 71.

Lecky, opinion cited in *Memoir* pp 317–8 as to the profound difference between cases of England and Ireland.

T F Tout, *France and England,* their relations in the Middle Ages and now (1922) p 102. With which compare Maitland, *Collected Papers* III 297–8.

E. *Knowledge and Action.*

In no respect is the value of sound knowledge to a statesman more evidently shewn than in the behaviour of leaders brought face to face with grave emergencies. By sound knowledge I mean such knowledge of the

past as helps a man to distinguish between real and
apparent values in considering the facts and prospects
of a present situation. Whether this knowledge is got
from books or from personal observation or from both
sources does not matter. Opportunities for applying it
are never lacking, but its usefulness is never more
plainly demonstrated than in cases where the continued
validity of traditions and principles is in question. Facts
may be so strong as to override theories based on earlier
facts. But, has the hour come for definite action steadily
directed to acceptance of a new theory based on the new
facts? That is the issue, heavily complicated for the
statesman by the necessity of carrying his people with
him. He has to judge them, as well as the rights and
wrongs of the situation. For failure (and without their
support he must fail) will surely leave things worse than
before. Imagination cannot depict the strain on a leader's
capacities in such a case.

It is tempting to cite as a notable instance the case
of the foundation of the Roman Empire by Augustus.
We may truly say that he read the signs of the times
aright, that he avoided dangerous pitfalls with subtle
skill, that he built a structure which lasted long; in short
that he remodelled the present with profound understanding of the past. Yet we feel a certain hesitation
to place him in the first rank of the world's heroes.
To some critics what we hear of his personal character
may serve to justify the doubt. But there is a more
serious objection in the fact that his achievement only
amounted to a reorganization sufficiently effective to

put off the evil day. It was not his fault that he could not give a fresh and genuine vitality to an empire such as he found it. Roman conquest and Roman administration had left no live forces capable of developing national units through internal growth; nor was it possible then to see that the future lay with national developments. And Roman citizenship did not mean the existence of a Roman nation. Therefore, great and lasting though the effect of his reconstruction was, it can hardly be cited as a happy instance in point. Nor, for various reasons, is it in general satisfactory to appeal to the critical judgments and decisions of leaders who, openly or in disguise, have wielded autocratic power.

The matter is best illustrated from the history of the United States. Washington had to determine his choice on very difficult considerations. He knew what the policy of the British government had been in the past. Was there good reason to believe that its recent tendency would be so reversed as to make possible a sincere return to the former state of things? He knew that the colonists had outgrown the stage of patient acquiescence, and that some colonies were ready to rebel. He knew that rebellion could only be justified by success. Would the colonies cooperate so effectively as to give a reasonable prospect of victory? If they won the day, what next? Union was strength, but, if success dissolved union, would not each isolated colony be at the mercy of foreign powers, and liable to be ruled as Canada had been by France? Was not the rule of Great Britain, who had removed the French menace, better than the risk of such a result? The problem was a complicated one, full of doubtful factors. That independence was the best solution became gradually clear to Washington. All then must turn on the prospects of military success. Now all Americans knew how in the Canadian campaigns British superiority in numbers had been turned to little account by British blundering. How self-satisfied and unintelligent British generalship could be, Washington had learnt thoroughly under Braddock. War in America was best understood by Americans. So he took the step never to be retraced. One thing turned out different from expectation; I mean the obstinacy of the British government controlled by George III. Hence the long duration of the war, and eventual victory gained only with the aid of France. But the situation had been rightly judged on the whole. Colonial cooperation had not been fatally broken during the war, though terribly strained, and in due course was converted into union.

Great though the work of Washington surely was, and well though he deserved to be called Father of his Country, the case of Abraham Lincoln is an even more striking instance from my present point of view. There is no need to sketch his achievements generally, when placed in a position perhaps the most trying that mortal man has ever had to face. No one can read his speeches, letters, official documents, not to mention his recorded sayings and private acts, without a feeling of amazement. Here was a man of what he called the 'plain people', untried in high office, suddenly put to the front, with the duty of guiding a great people in its time of supreme trial, even if the crisis involved civil war. The South openly repudiated him: in the North there was a strong minority opposed to the principles of which he was the chosen representative. Jealousy and bitter hostility lost no chance of putting the worst construction on his policy. He was denounced as misusing his powers: but, if to such judges he seemed to be going too fast and too far, to eager spirits of his own following his slowness and caution were at times an irritating strain on loyalty. Every disadvantage that attends the blessings of 'government of the people, by the people, and for the people', was present on a colossal scale in the agony of the greatest of all Democracies.

That Lincoln nevertheless performed his task, and that his decisions on almost every important issue have been approved by the judgment of posterity, we know. We are tempted to praise his commonsense and grit, and there to leave the matter. I am not content to do this. When we are considering the effect of knowledge and training on statesmen[1], a really good concrete illustration is a sheer godsend, and the case of Abraham Lincoln seems to furnish an illustration signally interesting and clear. From a childhood of illiterate poverty he raised himself through dogged industry to the position of a country lawyer; and lawyer he remained to the end of his life. His legal knowledge was never wide in a technical sense; but, painfully acquired for immediate use, it had

[1] The words of Lord Bryce in his introduction to *The Speeches and Letters* of A L (ed 1907) fully justify my use of the present illustration.

to be sound as far as it went. It is recorded of him that he always strove to promote agreement and discourage litigation, and that he early gained and kept the confidence of his neighbours. To deserve other men's trust seems to have been with him a steady motive to the last. Now, was not the practice of the law, by a man something far more than a mere lawyer, a most apt education for a statesman? Of the narrow mechanical views that are not seldom to be found in men engaged in legal practice we have most of us some experience. History will supply cases among public characters. But to a man mentally sound and morally able to stand on the truth that Law is made for Man and not Man for Law, legal study and practice may be the very best of training for public life.

Such was the position of Lincoln when he was called to deal with a situation of unexampled complexity. The political atmosphere was charged with legal debate on the question of State rights, and later authorities leave it by no means clear that on the formal ground of legality the South was in the wrong. In the recent controversy with Douglas, Lincoln had set forth his views. He was for maintaining the Union at all costs, and for preventing the extension of slavery; but he was opposed to any design of suppressing slavery where it already existed. To carry out this policy he had been elected President. His equipment for the purpose consisted first and foremost in a thorough and well-digested knowledge of the past history of the United States. From this he had learnt two main lessons; first, that the laws in force must not be broken[1] by the national Government; and secondly, that in practice the value of formal legality is inevitably lessened by the lapse of time. So he did not take arms to put down Secession until it appeared openly as armed rebellion: he did not gratify the Abolitionists by decreeing emancipation until events had shewn it to be a step necessary for the speedy ending of the war. History has justified him. His murder left his merits to be significantly illustrated by contrast, for in the hands of an ignorant and obstinate successor the chances of a great and glorious reconciliation faded away. He remains an inspiring example of the services that an honest and able man may render to his country by industriously qualifying himself for high responsibilities. Nor is it irrelevant to note that this child of penury and hand-labour could and did on solemn occasions raise public utterances to unrivalled dignity. And this by sticking to the point, and not tainting sincerity by display of rhetoric. What noble or fashionable statesman ever equalled the wholesome and lofty self-control of the little speech at Gettysburg?

Appendix F is a continuation of this, considering separately certain points that arise in connexion with the above topic.

---

[1] This is not belied by the arbitrary acts of the Executive during the war. They were submitted to as emergency measures, being felt to imply no real danger to constitutional freedom on the return of peace.

F. *Legality and Circumstance.*

The question, how far formal considerations of legality must be, and in fact are, overruled by changes of circumstance, is one of no small importance. We have ourselves a sad acquaintance with it in connexion with our Irish policy. But I think the best illustration of it is to be found in the story of American Secession. The leaders of that movement, in order to achieve their end, had naturally to hold out fair prospects of success. Now among these was the suggestion that what were then (1861) the Western States would be practically indifferent to the break-up of the Union, and so could not be relied on to support the Federal Government in maintaining it by force of arms. How many people genuinely believed this, we do not know: but it served the turn of partisans so to deceive others, and perhaps themselves. Starting with the assumption that the right of a State to secede was admitted by the language of the Federal Constitution rightly interpreted, a Secessionist could not understand why any one State, not being directly injured itself, or bent on dominating other States, should object to the exercise of a right equally open to itself should it so desire. Now this involved the further assumption that, in relation to the right in question, all the States stood on the same footing; in short, that the value of a reserved right to withdraw from the Union would carry the same weight in all States alike. If this were so, probably the Abolitionist section would find it no easy matter to draw the North-West into cooperation with the North on the common ground of opposition to slavery. That events belied this hope, and that even Kentucky could not be carried into Secession, we know.

Many causes in detail contributed to this result. But the most deep-seated, and from my present point of view the most interesting, may be stated as follows. All the original 13 States had free access to the Atlantic. On the supposition that they meant, in joining the Union, to reserve the right of leaving it if and when disposed to do so, they were assuredly viewing that possibility as it appeared to them in their own peculiar circumstances. If any State saw fit to resume independence, it would start with possession of a prime necessity, the free communication with the outside world. But as time went by, and new States were added to the Union, the position was silently changed. Most of the new States lay inland, and their communications with the world outside were not through ports of their own on the seaboard. Land-carriage eastward led through the Atlantic States: the way by the great lakes was dominated by Canada: the way by river was open, at least so long as New Orleans was in the hands of the Union. To the rapidly growing North-Western States Secession offered a poor prospect. None of them could gain by becoming an isolated unit, surrounded by what would then be foreign territory, and depending on foreign complaisance for communication with the outside world. And, even if the right to secede were legitimately deduced from the Federal Constitution, what State so situated would dream of asserting it? Secession would seem to them an unpractical folly. How could they sympathize with it as the policy of others? Their point of view was quite different from that of the Southern hot-heads on the question of State-rights pure and simple, and they knew that slavery alone had made that question a 'live issue'. So there was nothing to lessen a difference of feeling which was in fact fundamental.

To put this in other words, it is hardly too strong to say that, even assuming that the original conditions of the Union, fairly interpreted, left open the possibility of a voluntary withdrawal on the part of any State, the later development of the United States had made it practically impossible to allow the exercise of such a supposed right. The growth of new States of the Union did in fact tacitly assume that a certain extent of seaboard was a part of the national possessions. The triumph of Secession would have meant that half the Atlantic coast, the whole of the Gulf coast, and the Missisippi waterway, were henceforth to pass under the control of a foreign power. That inland States, loyal to the Union, would acquiesce tamely in such a result, no thoughtful man could really believe. The cry of 'State rights'; and protests against Federal interference with local liberties, might sound legal to slave-owners in South Carolina: it could not make free farmers in Ohio or Illinois willing to concede to others a privilege that they did not desire for themselves. On the legal issue opinions might differ; geography is a fact, and the rulings of geography are older and in the long run more effective than those of law.

That the Democratic party were strong in the (then) North western States, and that in 1862 the unfavourable course of the war had developed a serious opposition to the policy of Lincoln's government, is true. But the failure of Morgan's raid, owing to the hostility of the local population, clearly shewed that opposition to the present government did not mean sympathy with secession. Even verbal professions of sympathy with the South (and of such there was no lack) did not imply any willingness to make sacrifices for that cause. Circumstances were too strong. Therefore sentiments favouring peace only pointed to a peace based on the abandonment of the objects aimed at in the Northern States generally. The weakness of such a position is obvious. So the war went on. Gettysburg and Vicksburg turned the tide, and the national government found itself able even to enforce conscription.

Dr Rhodes points out (III 142) that in 1860 thoughtful men had seen that peaceable disunion was a geographical and military impossibility. On the situation in 1861 he says 'The Northwest believed this severance of the Union a blow to its own prosperity, perhaps depriving it of the important outlet of the Mississippi River for its products. The South, considerate of the West, now declared by its congress the free navigation of the Mississippi River (Feb 25). While one may note in the Southern literature of this period a particular animosity towards New England, there is evident a feeling of friendliness to the West, in some instances going so far as to express the extravagant hope that some

of the Western States might join the Southern Confederacy' (III 296). Later (IV 299) he remarks that in
1863, before the great development of the railroad
system, the control of the Mississippi was of more importance than it is now.

In his excellent little book *Division and Reunion*
(1893) Dr Woodrow Wilson refers to the relations of
South and West in the Union from 1829 onward, and
indicates the causes of their gradual change.

Professor W A Dunning in his *Essays on the Civil
war and Reconstruction* (1898) has an interesting discussion of the question, are the States equal under the
Constitution? He reviews the past history bearing on
this question, and decides that in theory they are not,
or were not at the time of writing. But in general public
opinion and in practice this is not so: the powers which
they do exercise are everywhere substantially the same
And there, without prophesying the future, he is content
to leave it (pp 304–352).

On the gradual change in American political theory,
by which the principle of Federalism (Hamilton) gained
ground at the expense of State-Rights (Jefferson), he
remarks that the latter school 'became identified with
a body of doctrine which in each successive decade
became more and more irreconcilable with objective
conditions. The constitutional dogma of state sovereignty
developed side by side with a growth in territory and
population and an increase in means of communication
which made steadily for nationalism' (p 358). In
connexion with this change he naturally treats of the

famous conflict of the two great leaders Webster and Calhoun.

M^r T Nelson Page, *General Lee* (1909) p 39, points out that when Lee was at the West Point Military Academy (he entered it in 1825) the text-books in use distinctly taught 'the absolute right of a State to secede, and the primary duty of every man to his native State'. He cites for this the authority of M^r C F Adams of Massachusetts, and further reminds the reader that the earliest instances of secession doctrine were of New England origin. This well illustrates what I have said as to circumstances overriding legality.

Col G F Henderson's *Stonewall Jackson* (ed 1902) contains a good discussion of the Secession issue and Jackson's view of his duty.

G. *The relativity of historical facts, as they present themselves for judgment.*

An act may be viewed in relation to the past (cause), or to the present (intention), or to the future (effect).

In the first case, the conclusion to be reached is simply its explanation as occurring in the circumstances of the time.

In the second case the choice of policy by the actor or actors at the particular juncture can be considered, and the responsibility of praise or blame can seldom be declined.

In the third case, the question is whether the action based upon the choice made at the given moment is justified or condemned by its results.

The distinction between these three points of view is evident when we reflect that a particular act may be (*a*) accounted for, (*b*) blamed in and for itself, (*c*) justified by the sequel, and yet form no precedent.

For to anyone seeking a precedent it must sooner or later become clear that in human affairs it is seldom or never possible to assign with confidence a particular effect to a single cause. A sequel is not always an effect, and other causes may have cooperated with the one that is most obvious. Therefore a suggested precedent is not a sound reason for present action.

If the historical verdict be that an act was in the given circumstances defensible or even praiseworthy, and yet led to bad results in the long run, precedent is clearly out of court, and moral judgment otiose.

The story of the Stuarts in the seventeenth century is full of striking illustrations of these points.

H. *Method—Forwards or Backwards?*

In the endeavour to grasp so far as possible the true story of past events with the view of training the political mind, we are faced by questions of method, one of which at least calls for some discussion. It is this—ought the student to work forwards, moving on from causes to effects, starting from some epoch arbitrarily chosen, or backwards, noting effects and then seeking causes? On the second plan the arbitrary choice of a starting-point raises no difficulty. The natural bent of a reader is no doubt to work forwards, but what about the serious inquirer? As historian he is the producer, while the ordinary reader is consumer.

It seems to me that the utterances of two great authorities, the late Bishop Stubbs and Professor Maitland, incidentally raise this question, and that the difference between them is rather apparent than real. Stubbs (*Lectures* pp 21, 29, 30, 102–4) is for the forward or synthetic method. But this is as a method for the teacher, and from that point of view it may perhaps be called necessary. That the backwards or analytic method is suited to men with little time at disposal, is not so easy to admit, at least as a method of study: for teaching it is hardly possible under ordinary conditions. Maitland touches the question in speaking (*Domesday Book and beyond* p 356, cf p 225) of the perils of anachronism, especially the intrusion of untimely ideas. He says 'The most efficient method of protecting ourselves against such errors is that of reading our history backwards as well as forwards, of making sure of our middle ages before we talk about the "archaic", of accustoming our eyes to the twilight before we go out into the night'. But this is a very general remark, and seems concerned with inquiry rather than with teaching. That the inquirer must be prepared to use both methods according to need may be accepted as final. That the teacher and the ordinary reader for various reasons cannot be expected to work backwards, seems a practical conclusion. Taking this position to start from, it may be worth while to look more carefully at the two methods and try to make out what are their respective advantages and disadvantages, supposing them to be separately followed.

The forward method is obviously more convenient, moving with the movement of time. As it moves on, it picks up a series of events, some of which are causes clearly contributory to the effects which may at first have seemed simply and solely due to some notable cause or causes already recognized. In other words, it is a check upon the fallacy of *post hoc ergo propter hoc*. At the same time it tends to become deductive and to exert a direct influence on future practice; that is, immediately to create in use a political Art. But it has to move on, and soon reaches a point at which situations, distant in time, have to be compared; and over the comparison it is apt to stumble, being apparently in possession of the whole truth. In practical politics this is liable to induce hasty inferences. For instance, it takes earlier events to account for later. But it is very liable to overlook some of the earlier, or to underestimate their value; and so to reason in a syllogism the minor premiss of which is of doubtful validity. The danger of hasty conclusions applied in practice is manifest. Now that situations do not recur exactly, seldom even approximately, is generally admitted. Phenomena do recur, but uncorrelated phenomena are not history. History is essentially the correlation of phenomena, and it is on this quality in full and watchful exercise that must rest whatever claim it has to be called a Science.

The backward method has one obvious merit, that it starts by ascertaining the result for which it attempts to account. This is a sound scientific beginning. The inquirer's eye is kept from the first directed on the task of discovering why the result in question came about. So far well. If a satisfactory stopping-point could be found, this method of working back from effect to cause would, though difficult, serve its purpose very well. In its backward course it will pick up contributory causes, hitherto insufficiently recognized or ignored, and become to a considerable degree inductive. In so far as its collected material is exact and its inferences logical, it may well claim the status of a Science. But it suffers heavily from attempting more than human powers can carry out fully. The bulk of detail, even when not increased by recent research, steadily expands as the inquirer moves backward. Suppose him to have reached a point at which he feels sure of his ground in proving the causes of a particular effect: by that time he will be beginning to feel uneasy as to precedent causes of which those direct causes were in their turn effects. He will have to move slowly, by reason of growing mass of detail. And, if he stops at some fixed epoch, he is conscious of an arbitrary choice, due perhaps partly to exhaustion.

It may be fair to conclude that the forward method is apt to end in hasty inference, and the backward method in a process *ad infinitum.*

I. *Comparative instructiveness of various national histories.*

That the histories of some peoples in some periods are more instructive from the statesman's point of view than those of other peoples, or of the same peoples in other periods, is hardly to be disputed. But I do not think that this fact always receives practical recognition. There is a tendency to fall into a groove, and certain histories (for instance, that of France) become so firmly established as material of training that others of not less value pass almost unregarded. A teaching staff has its limits, and men who specialize on certain peoples and periods inevitably see the importance of their own special subjects through magnifying spectacles. This is not to be blamed: it is only a mode of wholesome enthusiasm. Moreover it is partly favoured by considerations of scale. It is only natural that the affairs of peoples by whom a great state[1] has been formed, or who have for some long time played a leading or dramatic part on the world-stage, should attract particular attention. But it does not follow that the histories of such peoples are the most rich in political education for a student in a given country at a given time. Problems of statesmanship are ever changing, not only in detail, but in their general character. For instance, the relation between the State as a whole and its parts is a far more important issue now than it was one or two centuries ago. Federalist and Unitary principles are at work side by side, and questions arise that are difficult to answer and are answered differently. The experience of Federalism in the Western world is not always directly applicable to European conditions, operating as it has done in a vast open area and not being

[1] See H A L Fisher, *Studies in History and Politics* (1920) p 174, on the value of small States.

hampered by traditions of sympathy or antipathy from a long and troubled local past.

It may I think fairly be urged that the passage from feudal particularism to autocratic monarchy, once a subject of great interest, is no longer so important as to direct special attention to those histories in which that development is best illustrated. Important it will still be, of course, but of less interest than the study[1] of federal or quasi-federal relations. And this study would naturally, so far as Europe is concerned, be mainly directed to two States, the Swiss Confederation and the Dutch Netherlands. Of these two, there can be little doubt that the latter is the more interesting and instructive. The story of Switzerland, with its heroisms and the triumphs of patient wisdom over many difficulties, is calculated to arouse warm sympathy and respect. But admiration of an independence gallantly achieved, and a thrifty prosperity as soberly maintained, does not imply that much is to be learnt from Swiss experience. Isolated in the uplands far away from the sea, surrounded by states of larger population and resources, it cannot be overlooked that the Confederation owes its survival partly to the mutual jealousies of its great neighbours. It has never been a 'Great Power'; that is, it has never been exposed to the strain of carrying on a far-reaching and continuous foreign policy. And without that test it is not easy to say how far its solutions of internal problems offer lessons to statesmen of countries less peculiarly situated. The

[1] See C H Pearson, *National life and character* (1894), pp 235–6.

skill with which peoples of different races and languages have been welded together in an artificial but effective nationality is the great Swiss contribution to the instruction of the world. And, that this result has not been forwarded by the warnings of external pressure, it would be rash to affirm.

The Dutch Netherlands stand historically on a very different footing. The conquest of their independence was followed by a bold entry into the politics of the world. Industries, set going or kept vigorous by refugees from other lands, created astounding wealth at home and promoted a vast commerce abroad. For the greater part of the seventeenth century they had the chief share of the carrying trade; their fisheries were unrivalled, and their navy long the first of sea-powers. They won, and farmed to high profit, a rich colonial empire. In banking and finance they were accepted models. Religious toleration, in spite of some unhappy differences in course of time, made its first genuine appearance there. All studies made their home, and the arts reached an amazing development, in this flat uninspiring country. The Republic of the United Provinces was in short one of the Great Powers of Europe in its day of glory. But by the end of the seventeenth century other growing powers had detected its real weakness and were beginning to turn that weakness to their own advantage. Eager to extend commerce, the Dutch grasped lands beyond the seas, but did not expand their territory in Europe. Thus they had no large area from which to draw a native military force, and for protection of a very vulnerable frontier they had to rely on fortresses and mercenary armies. Their strength at sea rested on secure prosperity at home, and this was liable to destruction or disturbance by armed invasion. Once the menace became real, they depended on the support of allied powers for their own safety, and quickly sank into a subordinate position. By the end of the eighteenth century they had reached a stage of impotence and poverty so extreme that they counted for nothing. The sufferings and exhaustion of that miserable time would no doubt be painfully instructive; they deserve a full inquiry by a qualified Dutch historian, able to make the story clear to foreign readers. The revival since their fall has been a signal triumph of patience and thrift, and a fine example to all peoples that have been (or may be) exposed to a similar trial.

Now at the back of these striking phenomena there are notable facts that seem to have had much to do with this strange career of success and failure. An insufficient territorial basis of power was surely dangerous from the first. Expansion no doubt had its difficulties, but it did not need to involve forcible annexation. The seven Provinces had been united by community of interests to win freedom, but in their prosperity they made no serious effort to enlarge their territory by further confederations. To their sea-power, resting on wealth, they only added alliances with other powers from time to time, and they were often thwarted by the shortcomings of their allies. But sea-power, vastly important though it is, operates from a land-base, and can only prevail if that base offers secure and adequate resources. The naval wars with England applied a severe test. We ask, how came it that English inefficiency under Charles II was on the whole superior to Dutch skill, though the Dutch navy was led by the greatest admiral of the age? I think inquiry will find the main cause[1] in the political relations of the seven Provinces. The hindrances to effective co-operation, arising out of the attempt to work seven constitutions at once when unity was urgently required, deserve careful study. I know of no historic experience that illustrates so vividly the vital difference between local autonomy under a central government and jealous independence of sectional units. That the Province of Holland and the city of Amsterdam in the long run determined the course of national policy, is true; but at the cost of endless friction and delay. The Seven were not all hives of industry and commerce: they were hardly to be called a nation: and the rural Provinces were slow to follow without question the lead of a burgher aristocracy. The one continuous influence that was effective beyond Provincial boundaries was attachment to the House of Orange. But no real national unification took place until the country had passed through its hour of utter humiliation, and then only as the gift of foreign powers.

An inquiry into the working of the Union, with its tangle of Provincial governments on various models, the local jealousies that hindered cooperation and neutralized

---

[1] I am not here ignoring the fact that the shallowness of Dutch waters was a hindrance to the building of ships of deep draught.

the advantages of a compact territory, would surely be instructive. Hardly less so would be the financial failure at the end of the eighteenth century, when the famous Bank of Amsterdam, an accepted pattern of efficiency, collapsed. Closely bound up with the profits of colonial empire, the inability to retain that empire meant for the time simply ruin. Its restoration could not be, and was not, the result of Dutch exertions: what they have been able to do with the parts eventually restored shews that the people had not lost their patient energy. Out of the whole story will emerge the conviction that in their great age they were in fact attempting too much with resources too limited and too precarious, and relying too much on the money-power of a commerce that could not be permanently sustained. So far they did as others are perhaps now doing, and some decline was inevitable. But we may doubt whether it needed to be so extreme. It was the inner weakness of their Union government that left them helpless, the prey of aggressors, unable to stand alone, the derision of Europe. Their history presents a scene of constitutional defects never remedied under republican forms. There was no democracy to bear the blame of inefficiency. Merchant princes and local nobility went as blindly to their doom as did the nobles of Poland.

Surely this story, of which I have indicated a few points, is eminently deserving of the attention of modern students. The issues presented in its successive stages are not extinct problems arising out of conditions of purely antiquarian interest. Political, commercial, financial, they are still living issues, only modified in detail by the effect of time. As such, I submit that they deserve more attention from historical schools than they seem at present to receive.

As to the importance of American history from this point of view, I have said enough under other heads, and need not repeat it here.

K. *Body politic and body natural.*

In my remarks on this comparison I have particularly in view Mr Bateson's Herbert Spencer lecture delivered at Oxford in 1912. This, and the same author's Galton lecture, contain the most powerful statement of the political conclusions to be drawn from the analogy affirmed. Of the false doctrines, expressed or tacit, attacked in these striking papers, some had long before been discussed and condemned by Sir James Stephen in *Liberty, Equality, Fraternity* (ed II 1874). It is interesting to compare the methods by which the lawyer and the biologist reach very similar conclusions. As I do not think that either writer deals quite fully with human possibilities, or even human achievement, under present conditions, I cannot accept their pessimism at par. How the question presents itself to other writers is therefore to me a matter of some interest.

Prof J B Bury's essay *Darwinism and History* (in the Darwin centenary volume 1909) touches on this subject of the comparison of a society to an organism. In § 6 he refers to the views of Spencer and others, and remarks that a society has analogies with an organism, but is not an organism. In an organism the cells are morphologically as well as functionally differentiated, but in a society individuals are morphologically homogeneous and only differentiated functionally. This may be true and yet not contradictory to Mr Bateson's view. For it passes over the difference of quality in individuals, on which Mr Bateson lays the greatest stress in connexion with the doctrines of heredity.

Francis Galton, *Hereditary Genius* (ed 1914) p 350, speaking of typical characters in living beings, compared with the typical appearance always found in different descriptions of assemblages, says 'It is true that the life of an animal is conscious, and that the elements on which it is based are apparently unconscious, while exactly the reverse is the case in the corporate life of a body of men'.

It has often been observed that the 'mass' of a society is not merely the total formed by adding together all its members. Benedetto Croce *(Theory and history of historiography,* Eng trans 1921 p 105) restates this. The 'mass' is not a complex of individuals, but something else, which moves the mass of individuals. Right or wrong, this consideration seems at all events relevant in treating of society as an organism. Compare W R Paterson, *The Nemesis of nations* (1907) p 335, Hearnshaw, *Democracy at the Crossways* (1918) p 43.

S R Gardiner, pref to vol x (1884) p x remarks that there is 'a danger of regarding society as governed by external forces, and not by forces evolved out of itself. The statesman of the present wants perpetually to be reminded that he has to deal with actual men and women. Unless he sympathizes with them and their ideas, he will never be able to help them, and in like manner a historian who regards the laws of human progress in the same way that he would regard the laws of mechanics misses, in my opinion, the highest inspiration for his work'. Carefully considered, this seems to state on its practical side a part of the question to which the view of Mr Bateson offers an answer.

J S Mill, *Logic* v 5 § 6, on the Fallacy of false Analogies, rejects that between bodies politic and bodies natural. 'Decay of the vital powers in an animated body can be distinctly traced to the natural progress of those very changes of structure which, in their earlier stages, constitute its growth to maturity; while in the body politic the progress of those changes cannot, generally speaking, have any effect but the still further continuance of growth: it is the stoppage of that progress, and the commencement of retrogression, that alone would constitute decay. Bodies politic die, but it is of disease or violent death; they have no old age'. See also *ibid* vi 9 § 3, 10 § 3, 11 § 1.

Physiologists must judge that part of this utterance which belongs to their province. The political part seems to assert that change in the body politic is, unless violently interrupted, not organic, but rather a rearrangement of its constituent elements, a process continued indefinitely. If this view be correct, I presume that the phenomena of the 'body politic' are to be considered abstractedly, not in connexion with the fortunes of any particular society or the question of its continued identity under changing conditions.

Lord Morley, *Notes on politics and history* (1913) p 43 denies any true analogy between the body politic and the body natural, and holds that the methods and processes of politics are not to be brought within sight of those of biology. 'The politician may borrow phrases from the biologist, and talk of embryos, germs, organisms, but surely those are right who insist that we have not come near to the definite creation of an inductive political science'. He refers to Maitland's *Collected Papers* III 288.

This passage speaks for itself. But with it I would compare the words of Lord Bryce, *Studies* (1901) vol I p 309 'Neither can we foresee the modes in which the scientific way of looking at all questions may come ultimately to tinge and modify men's habits of thought even in social and political matters'.

Interesting too is the regret expressed by Renan in his *Recollections of my youth* (Eng trans 1883) at having been led to devote himself to the historical sciences (*petites sciences conjecturales*), which are no sooner made than they are unmade, rather than to Chemistry Astronomy Physiology etc.

In J R Seeley's *Introduction to Political Science* (1896) the analogy is most fully accepted, indeed much seems to rest on it. But it was published after his death, and may not be his last word.

H G Wells, *First and last things* (ed 1917) pp 36–8, speaking of the use of the term 'Science' in connexion

with the study of human affairs, argues to this effect.
'Science' in usage does connote certitude, but the science
of society stands at the extreme end of the scale from
the molecular sciences. To compare societies with
animals is misleading. The method of classification under
types cannot be used in social science. 'This denial of
scientific precision is true of all questions of general
human relations and attitude'. Cf *ibid* p 164.

Arnold Toynbee, *Industrial Revolution* (ed 1908) distinguishes forcibly between the laws of physical and social
science. The latter 'express, for the most part, facts of
human nature, which is capable of modification by self-
conscious human endeavour'. pp 160, 170, 246, 271.

E Jenks, *The State and the Nation* (1919) pp 9, 11.
'A society is not an organism, because its members have
each a distinct individuality, which the parts of a true
organism have not, and because it has no consciousness,
as distinct from the respective consciousness of its
members'. . . . . 'a real danger in speaking of the State
as a conscious being'—with human passions. And on
p 136 'The writer has never claimed to enunciate laws
of social development which operate with the mathematical precision of inanimate Nature. The moral
sciences, unlike the physical sciences, are statements
only of *normal*, or average, tendencies. They are true in
the given circumstances, though not universally. They
represent *tendencies*, not, necessarily, accomplished facts'.

W Pitt, in a speech quoted in Payne's edition of
Burke vol 1 p xlv, gave a popular version of a similar
argument.

Ernest Scott, *Men and thought in modern history* (1920) p 118 gives an interesting quotation from Bentham on the point. And on p 199 there is a protest against the *non possumus* of H Spencer's Individualism.

H W C Davis, *The political thought of H von Treitschke* (1914) pp 128–30 cites Treitschke's protest against such analogy as being lazy fatalism.

But the fullest and most direct treatment of this matter is to be found in an essay on *The body politic* by Professor F W Maitland (*Collected Papers* vol III). He held that the analogy might be useful in the way of suggestions. It would enrich the vocabulary of historians and political theorists, particularly in respect of metaphors. And this would supply not only new phrases but new thoughts. But at present it is not well for the student of history to hand himself over to the professor of any one science. Our inductive political science has not yet reached a sufficiently high level of knowledge of social phenomena, nor does it seem likely to do so. That all states or nations are mortal in the sense that they have a natural (not violent) death, is a proposition to which he cannot assent. He cannot think of any instance in which the disappearance of a political organism of a high type could rightly be thus described. As to method of inquiry, he has much misgiving. Sociologists have not fully grasped the interdependence of human affairs, for example that of political religious and economic phenomena. Hence history suffers. There is too often an attempt to obtain a set of 'laws' by the study of only one class of phenomena. Conclusions reached by such detachment, e g the inductions obtained by study of barbarians, are too hasty: under severe historical criticism they are seen to prove far less than was supposed. We have no materials apt for such an induction, no means of forming the idea of the *normal* life of a body politic. Changes due to imitation in bodies natural are trivial compared with those in bodies politic. English trial by jury was copied by many other countries, at first minutely. Deliberate copying is seldom quite a success, often a failure. But the original position can never be restored. Changes in the body natural are not really comparable. Should we regard the whole progressive body of mankind as a single organism—and as infected by the strange disease called civilization? A science of bodies politic which knows nothing of normal or abnormal is a science falsely so called. Therefore 'Political Science' is a bad title. Students of history are not to be encouraged at present to aim at wider generalizations.

L. *Looking ahead—Lothrop Stoddard on the coming racial crisis.*

I have said in the Preface that History, working for the training of statesmen and citizens, will have to keep an eye on the imminent as well as on the past. This may seem to be a paradox, but in truth there has now for some years been present a cause of anxiety to thoughtful observers, usually expressed in the phrase Yellow Peril. Most men, to whom the urgencies of the present allow small leisure, ignore or try to ignore the menacing problem implied in the words, or lay it for the moment to rest by comforting assurances the validity of which they take no trouble to ascertain. Yet there are past and present phenomena that supply means of testing opinion and may lead at least to provisional conclusions. If it should appear[1] that the conditions of the modern world are favourable to a resurgence of the yellow and brown races of Asia, so that their economic and procreative competition threatens to overcome and submerge the hitherto superior white race, there is food for serious thought. And serious thought is useless save as a stage on the road to a judicious policy. Therefore those who study the past as a story of causes and effects need no excuse for keeping an eye on such an imminent problem as this.

It is significant that the reality of the problem and speculations as to its possible solution find most active expression in America. The absorption and assimilation of immigrants is a concern to the United States on a scale previously unknown in the world. Immigration is now ruled and restricted by law. This is not a mere blind jealousy, the fruit of a justifiable national pride. It has two aims; first, the exclusion of 'undesirable' elements; secondly, the allowance of sufficient time for assimilative agencies to operate with effect. Prejudice has no doubt had its say. But the most important aspect of the movement is the scientific endeavour, if not to assure the peopling of the country with the best stocks, at least to prevent its wholesale occupation by the worst.

[1] This question is treated at length in Dr Stoddard's book *The new world of Islam* (1921).

Europe and Asia offer boundless supplies of cheap labour, but this points to a state of things in which the standard of living would be permanently lowered. To this the American will not submit—not if he knows it—and who can blame him? With modern means of transit, shifting millions of men easily from land to land, is it not natural that the United States should be the first to take alarm?

Now, when an American sets himself to deal with great issues, he seldom leaves much room for mis-understanding of his views. Certainly there is no beating about the bush in two books by Dr Lothrop Stoddard[1], of which it is necessary to speak. *The rising tide of Color against White world-supremacy* (1920) and *The revolt against Civilization* (1922) are as plain as plain can be. The thesis of the former is that the yellow and brown peoples, never more than sullenly acquiescent in white domination, have gained increased self-consciousness and a feeling of common interest. The immediate cause of this was the Russo-Japanese war, inspiring hopes that by the use of Western means and methods the Oriental peoples might shake off the yoke of the West and go their own ways uncontrolled. That this has been and is their real wish is proved by ample evidence: the defeat of Russia removed the fear of Western military superiority, on which alone white domination rested. Pacific the masses of China and India may be; still

[1] Among the many authorities referred to by this author the book of Meredith Townsend, *Asia and Europe* (1901, fourth ed 1911) is well worth careful perusal.

their military power, if duly organized, would be enormous; and Islam with its warlike traditions is not to be forgotten. The teeming millions of yellow and brown races, whose fecundity outruns the highest of death-rates, need room to expand. Now they can live and thrive in climates where the white man can only be a sojourner, and can retain their working efficiency on food that would mean starvation to the white. Their output is greater than his, in proportion to the cost. In unrestricted competition they are able to beat him by 'underliving' him. White employers, looking only to immediate gain, will use (and have used) their services to make fortunes, and thus displace white labour. Meanwhile white philanthropists are eager to teach their Eastern brethren Western hygiene and reduce their death-rate. On this showing it appears that the situation is likely to become steadily worse for the white race, since by their own policy they are actively undermining their own former predominance.

It is tempting to reply that the picture is overdrawn. At present (1923) the state of things in China is by all accounts one of utter disorganization, and offers no prospect of real revival and development of power, at least within any measurable time. That Japan will gain control of China, and direct its vast resources against the interests of the Western world, is rather a nervous forecast than a serious probability. That the calm and just treatment of Indian affairs by Great Britain will not succeed in gradually training the native peoples to methods of peaceful and happy self-government, is an unjustified assumption. Nor is there at present reason to believe that the Islamitic world is in a position to lead an effective movement of revolt against European influences. In short, the drift of things is not so alarming as to encourage pessimism. But Dr Stoddard would no doubt answer that to argue thus is to take insufficient account of time. We must not judge the time-standards of the East by those of the West. The habit of many centuries has taught the East the power of waiting. The expansion of European influence and conquest in the East is but a thing of yesterday, and belongs to a period in which the Western peoples were fast growing in population and enjoying a monopoly of the strength derived from new inventions. So long as the vital forces of Europe remained unimpaired, the Oriental sullenly bowed to the inevitable. But, in addition to the Japanese victory over Russia, other things have completely changed the situation. Population no longer advances by leaps and bounds in Europe, and the effects of the great war have fatally reduced the strength of Western nations as a whole. Modern inventions are nowadays available[1] for the service of all the world. Granting that no immediate revolt of Asia is likely, is it likely that keen Asiatic wits, mostly resentful of Western patronage, are not laying these changes of circumstance to heart?

It may be said that moral conquest is more lasting than force, and that as Western ideas penetrate the East the old antipathy will die away and reconciliation based

[1] The significance of this fact was clearly foreseen by Benjamin Kidd, *Social Evolution*, ed 1898 p 248.

on common aims will make East and West work together in a blessed harmony of peace. But those Westerners who have lived long in the East do not encourage us to put faith in this alluring dream; nor do recent happenings in India and Egypt point that way. I fear it is only too true that the Oriental peoples, differing widely in so many other respects, have an inward bond of sympathy in common dislike of Western interference. And the vital powers of European peoples are not under modern conditions sufficient either to maintain it by force or to make it effective by pacific injection of moral influences. In short, political action of either kind is likely to become less and less. At certain points in certain ways time may be telling in favour of Western ideas: on the whole it is telling against them.

But after all this is not the main point of the problem in view. Dr Stoddard insists first and foremost on the fact that in human affairs the basic factor is not politics but race. Now, whatever hopes may be entertained of the effect of the infusion of Western influences into the East, and of attainment of a world-wide human harmony thereby, they must rest on the probable operation of one or both of two processes. One is the transformation of Orientals, mentally and morally, the breaking of immemorial tradition and habit, the shedding of a psychic heritage that has made them what they are. Of such a result there is not the faintest prospect; nor, if there were, is there any reason to suppose that good would come of it. The other is a dim notion at the back of some minds that diversity of race is not a fundamental truth of humanity. Races may blend, and new types, possibly valuable, may emerge from the fusion of blood: we had better do nothing to hinder a process which for all we can tell may be working towards a beneficent end. To the American this is sheer nonsense at best; at its worst, race-treason. It is nonsense, because the cross-breeding of different race-stocks does not produce a true blend. One or other of the factors is always prepotent, and the result is a mere mechanical mixture. The mongrels retain distinct race-characters, and in the course of generations the tendency is for these race-characters to re-differentiate, and so to emerge as pure types, representing the prepotent factor. Hence the danger of inferiors replacing or degrading superior stocks. It is race-treason, because the apathy of some and the immediate profit-seeking of others may let in a flood of alien immigrants. Economically irresistible, these will outwork (or rather *underlive*) white labour and check the growth of pure white population: if inter-breeding follows, they will destroy the white race altogether.

That the white race, particularly its 'Nordic' element, drawn from the northern parts of Europe, is superior to other stocks, and that it is well worth while to spare no pains in keeping it strong and uncontaminated, is only the natural conclusion of these views. And there is no way to save it other than exclusion of alien inferior stocks from 'white' countries. From this conclusion Dr Stoddard does not shrink. Citing some notable instances of the effects of immigration and interbreeding elsewhere, he boldly deals with the case of the United States. The early settlers, and their followers down to about the middle of last century, were indeed a chosen people. The high average of bodily moral and mental qualities was due to the practical working of eugenic selection, and a marked capacity for self-government was inherited from historic England. Non-British immigrants were almost all 'Nordic' Europeans, who blended well with the British majority. But in the last half-century a flood of less highly qualified immigrants has been pouring in from eastern and southern Europe, alien in race, of a much lower grade of civilization, more and more lowering the moral and political standards of the American people. The assimilation of these alien masses is proving to be a more difficult matter than easy-going politicians may have thought. Even economically they are a cause of some uneasiness. At first exploited as cheap labour, they are, now numerous enough to be a source of labour-troubles, and in politics their influence is mischievous.

Such in rough outline is the message of this book. In the second work, the *Revolt*[1], we have the same doctrine driven home and enforced by a further study of the race-problem as illustrating and explaining the perils which the author sees threatening the existence of civilized society. It has a second title, *The menace of the under-man*, in which its thesis is plainly expressed. Western civilization is in pressing danger from the

[1] I must say that this book seems to me inferior to the earlier one both in statement and in argument.

growing discontent of the classes whom our present
social system has placed (and keeps) on a low level,
while entrusting them with a power of which they are
becoming more and more conscious. At any moment
they may rise and annihilate the constructive results of
centuries in a sudden and general ruin. Recent phenomena occurring in many countries are cited to shew
that the picture is not overdrawn. Soviet Russia is merely
a specimen on an exceptionally large scale. The menace
is in being all over war-exhausted Europe: its full
seriousness is grasped when we realize that it has reached
that richest product of the modern world, the United
States of America. Even there may be detected signs
that inferior and degenerate elements are formed or
forming. In Europe the Proletariate are ready to smash
the irksome framework of society and to revert to the
congenial levels of chaotic barbarism or savagery. What
will come of this ferment, none can tell. It is at least
high time for America to take measures to guard against
so terrible a danger before it is too late. And recent
U.S.A. legislation seems to prove that Dr Stoddard is
not a voice crying in the wilderness. The immigration
laws shew a determination not to let administrative
slackness do irremediable harm by degrading the population of the States.

The question at once faces us, how could civilized
peoples allow themselves to drift into such a position
as this? After long ages of experience, had they learnt
no wisdom? Where are we to find the cause of their
error? For error there must surely be. The answer of

Dr Stoddard is that a civilization depends on the quality of its supporters. To keep that quality on a high level is the first duty of any people that intends to play a great and worthy part in the world. Nature makes no two beings exactly equal; in fact inequality is a law of nature, and inequalities are the more marked the higher you go in the biological scale. Evolution is not a movement towards equality. But for a long while past human policy has rested on a tacit assumption that diversities of races and individuals are mainly due to differences of environment. If so, they will be subject to modification through environmental change, and there is no need for the hampering assumption that the human race is divided by deep-seated, in fact fundamental, differences of character. Education and better surroundings will do wonders: these are the things that really matter. Of course no one openly asserts that you can gather grapes of thorns or figs of thistles. No stock-breeder acts upon the principle that it makes no odds whether you breed from good strains or bad ones. But in practice the one recognized distinction is that between mankind and the rest of living animals. That human types differ enormously and that the history of mankind is a product and a record of that difference, is simply ignored. In the soil of this slovenly ignorance an evil weed grows,— the vain delusion expressed in the claim of 'equality', the cry for which is fiercer than ever. The fallacy underlying this claim has only been exposed by modern Science, Biology in particular. No wonder then that revolutionary leaders are hostile to Science.

It is the ignorance or neglect of the true principles of heredity as connected with, and profoundly affecting, the course of human affairs, that is at the back of these phenomena. On the new doctrine no more need be said here, as I have said enough on other pages. Suffice it that the author takes it as proved by recent investigations, and urges that in future public policy must start from the assumption that Heredity is the basic factor of Eugenics, and Environment only an indirect secondary factor. Only eugenic reform can remedy the deep-seated disease of our civilization. Any mere tinkering with symptoms will leave the real cause untouched. As to actual measures, the beginning should be made by checking the reproduction of 'defectives', and so on, in the way usually proposed by eugenic reformers. But Dr Stoddard does not shirk the obvious question, by what power are you going to introduce this salutary change? He is well aware that the masses do not move by reason, and that their prejudices will have to be overcome by the vigour of a small enlightened minority. This consideration however does not daunt him. He truly remarks that in practice whatever has been achieved by human effort has been the work of dynamic minorities: the experiences of England France and Russia are instances enough. The present world-wide menace is itself everywhere the work of very few. But, if things are allowed to run their course unchecked, nobody can tell how fast the revolutionary propaganda may spread in the disastrous conditions left by the great war. Therefore there is no time to lose, if Western civilization is to be saved, and the white man is not to go under by his own fault and world-control to pass into the hands of other races.

The situation depicted in these energetic books may be, and probably is, not quite so grave as the author represents. But the news appearing day by day in the papers is enough to shew that there is much truth at the back of his pessimistic views and that his warnings are not safely to be ignored. At the same time we should not forget that there are in being forces capable of some resistance to recognized or presumed evils. Whether Prohibition or careful Control is the wiser method of dealing with the drink-problem, opinions may differ. How far racial duty requires a free people to turn back miscellaneous immigrants from their doors, overcoming the scruples of their own humanitarianism, is a matter for each people to decide. But the acts of the American government at least shew that they are conscious of their own power, and are at need prepared to use it. They do not mean to drift. The Home government of Great Britain seems less watchful and less bold: true, their position is much more difficult. If and when they do set themselves to face facts, it will probably be under the stimulus of the Dominions. The slackness of our policy in such a matter as Vaccination is certainly not reassuring. How to strengthen the hands of our rulers in dealing with great social issues is an urgent question; and it will hardly be answered successfully until we find a way to reconcile Labour-policy with the doctrines of Science. The coming Crisis may develope slowly. But is it not wiser, in view of the present and the recent past, deliberately to face the imminent, rather than to wait until immediate and irresistible pressure drives us to measures of defence crudely conceived in frantic haste? Is it not true that in order to reserve for the white race the vast territories of the British empire, the white must occupy them and not merely control them? And does not the possibility of such expansion abroad depend on the racial effect of improvement at home? Do not the changes of the last half-century, historically viewed, point to this conclusion and suggest that slovenly optimism is a deceptive guide? Can any inquirer, used to tracing the relations of cause and effect, shirk the duty of keeping such momentous issues to the front in politics?

M. *Madison Grant on the passing of the Great Race.*

In the chorus of warning voices from America none sounds more loud and clear than that of Madison Grant. His book, *The passing of the Great Race* or *The racial basis of European history*, reached a fourth edition in 1921. It is 'an attempt to elucidate the meaning of history in terms of race', and it sternly fulfils the promise of its title.

Starting from the scientific doctrine of Heredity, he regards modern social and political phenomena from the same point of view as other inquirers, and arrives at the same pessimistic conclusions. But as to remedies he is more explicit. A definite policy may be extracted from the book, consisting of (a) leaving the high birth-rate of the lower classes to be offset by a normally high death-rate, (b) sterilization of 'undesirables', (c) exclusion of low-type immigrants, and (d) apparently, fighting alcoholism as a bane of the highest (or Nordic) race.

Underlying this policy are two main principles. First, the superior human stocks have a right, indeed a duty, to save themselves from being bred out. All necessary means must be used to this end. Secondly, since you cannot induce the superior stocks to breed more freely under present conditions, the only alternative is to check the increase of the inferior. This applies to the case of any country that desires to avoid the permanent degradation of its people and government. For the results of past indifference to facts, and a philanthropy based on fallacies, are already alarming, and surely point to worse things to come.

The deadliest fallacy is the blind belief in the power of environment, the notion that good circumstances of life, nurture education and so forth, can make any sort of man into a good man and a good citizen. Connected with this is the assumption that interbreeding of two types produces a true blend of their several qualities on equal terms. Now here are two errors, as false as false can be. Science has at least proved this much, that environment, though helping or hindering survival, cannot change the fixed character: and that interbreeding produces mongrels, generally of poor quality from the first, and tending in course of generations to revert to the character of the inferior type. That these facts are in practice ignored by the most highly civilized peoples, is certain; also, that whole populations, particularly in America, are in danger of a change of character so complete that their identity may disappear, and all the achievements that made them what they are may thus be lost for ever.

The prospect suggested by these considerations is indeed such as to justify alarm. It is in effect the same as that set out in the other books referred to above, and this writer seems to have been first in the field, the initiator of the present campaign to revive race-consciousness. He takes the lead in boldly challenging the influence of religion and philanthropy as a cause of the social evil now menacing the stability of civilization. Their theories, expressed or implied, favour the multiplication of inferior stocks through their well-meant efforts to reduce the death-rate, which is the only effective check on excessive increase. So far the danger is one arising from the present population. But it is greatly enhanced by the action of capitalist employers, who are gainers by cheap labour, and encourage unrestricted immigration of foreigners inferior to the natives in social and physical standards. For the sake of a passing economic profit they are thus lowering the mental moral and bodily average of the American people. This danger arises from importation of persons unfit to share the privileges and duties of a great race. The capitalist invites them for his own ends, the philanthropist nurses them on altruistic principles, the politician courts them as voters, and the time is fast approaching[1] when these inferior races will be the real *populus Americanus*. The claim to be treated as the equals of the race that won by its own merits the opportunities now enjoyed by all alike is not one likely to be abandoned by those who have everything to gain by it.

Now the whole notion of Equality is a poison that has long vitiated political thought. Science can find no support for it: Inequality is nature's rule. Altruistic attempts to nullify this are artificial, and a waste of energy. Religions are largely responsible for the errors of thought and action. The professors of any creed can hardly escape having some special sense of community with those whom they regard as the Faithful. This influence, extreme in Islam, is also powerful in the various schools of Christianity. It operates, and has long operated, in defiance of what Science proclaims to be the laws of nature. If we are to follow the argument of Madison Grant and others to its logical conclusion, it would seem that the elimination of religious influences ought to be one of the most effective steps towards the recovery of racial consciousness and the maintenance of the Great Race wherever it exists. Probably the author would disown this inference put in so crude and brutal a form. But it is at least clear on his showing that existing religious influences and scientific principles as

---

[1] A highly qualified American citizen lately told me that he took some comfort from the fact that most of the foreign undesirables settle in cities and are subject to the effect of high death-rate. See books named on page 164.

at present understood are in conflict. One or other must either give way or be so modified as to change the character of its claim on the obedience of mankind.

Here is, I think, an issue that must be faced—the old story of Human Nature. Is there such a thing, however hard to define, still sufficiently recognizable, and in fact recognized, to affect human judgments, human motives, and consequently human action? If there is not, what course is open but to submit passively to what are called Nature's Laws, that is the competitive scramble in which living creatures, using the opportunities of place and time, survive by destroying their rivals? This means the abandonment of civilization, of all the restraints that mankind have imposed on themselves, of all the liberties and privileges that they have gained by exercise of such restraints. If on the other hand Human Nature is a reality, if it stands for something not shared by other animals and plants, surely we must try however feebly to form some notion of the difference asserted. If Man is the 'lord of creation', by what qualities has he attained this preeminence? May we not say that the power of intelligent combination, and the power of continuously learning by recorded experience, have been two of the chief factors? And do not these imply self-restraint, the check on momentary impulses? Are not humanitarian influences and scruples of many kinds a development along the same lines? As to religion, if it began by being a family or tribal bond, the mark of an assumed blood-relationship, it has long outstepped those limits, and has taken more humanitarian forms Can we, in considering the future welfare of the human race, rule out religious, philanthropic,—in a word, altruistic—influences as mischievous? If they are manifestations of the long-continued resistance of mankind to natural laws that have made other species what they are, should we be in haste to condemn them? Roughly, is Humanitarianism a part of human nature, or not?

If we answer that, however we account for its growth, it is now in fact a part, we shall have to make allowance for it at every turn. That is to say that 'eugenic' measures of all sorts will be limited by the scruples that humanity will openly or tacitly prescribe. And the problem of finding and keeping in operation a procedure at once humane and effective will be one of extraordinary difficulty. Political fluctuations will not cease because at some given moment the party in power has made up its mind. Humanitarian scruples will not be extinguished in a hurry, and will remain at the service of reactionary movements. These considerations amount to a recognition of the purely practical obstacles. If on the other hand we hold that human nature does not include Humanitarianism, and that this influence may be disregarded as an irrelevant and perhaps unwholesome development, eugenic reformers would seem free to go ahead with their projects. Once in the seat of power, they can so direct the generative process of nature on scientific lines as to save the residue of the Great Race, indeed to recreate it by natural and stable increase. But this policy, however justifiable, would be an act of force,

and as an act of force it must be judged. Will it not
have to be judged by its consequences, and what are
those consequences likely to be? Here we are up against
the root-problem of the whole matter.

Let us suppose that eugenic reform has advanced so
far in a country that its superior stock is numerically
strong and effectively dominates its policy. What
guarantee is there that this stock will be able, century
after century, to withstand the influences that have
been the ruin of other Great Races in the past? There
will be no superior power to control it from without:
what power is there to fortify it against creeping
maladies within? That the ruling classes of great states
have fallen from their high estate and passed away, is
a commonplace of history duly recognized by Mr Grant.
That it has been the result of internal decay in some
form or other, is in most cases generally admitted. The
causes and phenomena of the decay may vary in detail
and degree: but there appears one main cause ruthlessly
operative in all cases, though the modes of its working
may exhibit a superficial difference. This is the temptation to enjoy fully the opportunities of ease offered by
the tenure of power. The ruling class, dominant through
their energy and virtues, devolve all hard manual labour
on their subjects. For themselves, either they remain a
warrior aristocracy, whose ranks are thinned by losses
in war, or they degenerate in unmeaning idleness, or
they hasten their own ruin through their own feuds and
quarrels. The true story of mankind seems to be this:
a race that will not labour with its hands is on a road

that does not lead to survival. By the exercise of wise judgment and self-control, by evidence of great public services, it may long retain its prestige. But all the while some families are dying out, and new ones not of the pure race have to be admitted to the ruling class. Otherwise, its extinction is only a question of time. Meanwhile, hardened and trained in wholesome virtues by the necessities of toil, the hewers of wood and drawers of water survive and multiply. In the course of generations they steadily gain ground on their masters: a stream of competent recruits passes from their ranks into the upper class, gradually modifying it. Are we compelled to believe that such modification must always be for the worse?

The answer to this seems to depend on the value assigned to the upper class, racially considered, in comparison with the other (presumably lower) stocks. Mr Grant finds his American Great Race in the native Americans descended from the very select immigrants of the colonial period. We need not quarrel with this conclusion. But he insists that the early settlers were practically all of 'Nordic' stock, and that the 'Nordics', as compared with 'Alpines' and 'Mediterraneans', are beyond all doubt a superior race. In manly and governing qualities, as fighters and rulers, I think he makes his case good. Nor need we dispute the assertion that what we roughly label as 'progress' in human affairs is mainly due to the work of North-European stocks. But perhaps this is not all. He has to admit that much of what we call Civilization comes from the other groups, particularly the 'Mediterranean'. And, in order to justify the claim of Nordic superiority, he is led to discuss the races of Europe (indeed of the world) in a sketch, anthropological, somatological, psychological, of their various characteristics and past history, from the earliest appearance of the human species on the earth. Evidence, cranial, linguistic, technical, is diligently summoned from every quarter. And the mass of material is most impressive.

It is when the reader notices the reservations, limitations, and frank assertions of probability, on the honest writer's part, that he becomes uneasy. In this atmosphere of piecemeal fact interpreted by ingenious hypothesis is there now a solid basis for the very definite and far-reaching conclusions of the treatise? I say 'now', because I admit that another (say) hundred years of research may establish these conclusions, or others not less wide. It is hardly likely that the evidence, expanded and sifted, would then justify exactly the same inferences as are drawn at present. For even now doctors disagree on many points. Therefore I doubt whether present views, even undisputed, will undergo no change. To push forward thorough investigations, to coordinate the results in provisional hypotheses as a means of testing and suggestion, is a scientific procedure. But great caution is needed in using such material for the purpose of solving immediate problems,—even racial problems— calling for action, it may be for action of momentous consequence.

That the upper classes in Europe, and in the United

States also, are a good deal 'mixed', is not denied by the author of the book before us. And this alone is enough to give us pause before assenting to his positive doctrine and believing in the efficacy of his scheme for saving and multiplying the Great Race, the aristocracy of America. To restore, or rather recreate, a valuable stock may be possible by an arbitrary legislative policy of restricted immigration, such as is already being put in practice. But surely, the better the quality of the immigrants, the more they or their children will tend to rise and become important members of the great nation still in the making. If the native citizen of the past, in the quest of wealth, too heedlessly imported cheap labouring hands of low racial type, and is now in peril from their fast-growing numbers; is it not likely that now, by admitting only a select quota, he will more slowly but as surely be raising up generations of higher quality, who will unavoidably share his primacy? What harm if they do, it may be asked? Perhaps none, from the all-human point of view. Mixture will follow, but the Great Race will be a somewhat different Great Race. To one so convinced as Mr Grant that the only racial purity worth having is 'Nordic' racial purity such a prospect is of course disgusting. But, if the Nordics are already mixed, what else is there to hope for? If they persist in race-suicide and ease, yet would like to survive, had they not better mix with some who will both work and breed, and so achieve (say) a 50 per cent survival?

It is indeed not easy for one living in the atmosphere of slow-moving English ideas to appreciate the seriousness of the situation that so disturbs the American observer and leads him to advocate such drastic measures. That a systematic exclusion of 'undesirables' is wise, few will deny. We may even wish that the same policy were thoroughly carried out in Great Britain. But that this would be the saving of our 'Great Race', maintaining it in its racial character as at present existing, is not at all clear. Our upper class has been and is subject to change, and so it pretty certainly will be. It has had to adapt itself to changes of the times. So far as it survives, it is through its own energy and its refusal to despair. Recruited from time to time by foreign elements, it absorbs them and goes its way. What better could it do? It works. It even supplies a number of active pioneers to open up new lands. No doubt it has a good share of that 'ruthless concentration on self-interest' which Mr Grant finds so objectionable a quality in Polish Jews. No doubt it does not lack the 'intense individualism' which he admires in the Americans of a century ago. In short, it has its faults and its virtues, often but two sides of the same quality. So, in democratic circumstances, it contrives to hold its ground better than pessimistic grumblers will admit.

Only Americans themselves can form a sound judgment of American problems. The saying of Professor H F Osborn, 'We shall save democracy only when democracy discovers its own aristocracy as in the days when our Republic was founded', forcibly expresses the desire of a true patriot to make the government of the people in effect the government of its best elements.

A fine aspiration. If the most generally educated of peoples, in the most favourable circumstances ever known, cannot achieve this, who can? Are not some American patriots impatiently ready to make premature confession of their own impotence? Do they really think, Heredity notwithstanding, that the methods of the stock-yard are the only way to avert the Passing of the Great Race?

NOTE—Some other books of interest in connexion with the subjects of Appendices L and M.

(1) B L Putnam Weale, *The conflict of Colour*, 1910. Rather harsh and sometimes paradoxical, but often instructive, and full of warnings to England.

(2) Carl Becker, *The United States, an experiment in Democracy*, 1920. A strong book.

(3) John R Commons, *Races and Immigrants in America*, 1907. A manly book.

(4) F J Warne, *The Tide of Immigration*, 1916. A painstaking effort to state the case fairly.

INDEX OF NAMES OF AUTHORS OR CHARACTERS CITED OR REFERRED TO IN THE TEXT OR NOTES

The numbers refer to pages

For EU product safety concerns, contact us at Calle de José Abascal, 56–1°, 28003 Madrid, Spain or eugpsr@cambridge.org.